Kindergarten

Everyday Mathematics®

Program Guide and Masters

Kindergarten

Everyday Mathematics®

Program Guide and Masters

**The University of Chicago
School Mathematics Project**

Mc Graw Hill **Wright Group**

The *McGraw·Hill* Companies

UCSMP Elementary Materials Component

Max Bell, Director

Authors

Jean Bell, UCSMP
Max Bell, UCSMP
Dorothy Freedman,
    formerly of The University of Chicago Laboratory Schools
Nancy Guile Goodsell (First Edition)
Nancy Hanvey,
    formerly of Kozminski School, Chicago
Kate Morrison,
    formerly of The University of Chicago Laboratory Schools

Photo Credits

Phil Martin/Photography
Cover: Bill Burlingham/Photography
Photo Collage: Herman Adler Design Group

Contributers

Penny Stahly, Izaak Wirszup, Deborah Arron Leslie, Nancy Roesing

 **Wright Group**

Send all inquiries to:
Wright Group/McGraw-Hill
P.O. Box 812960
Chicago, IL 60681

ISBN 0-07-584432-X

4 5 6 7 8 9 10 11 BCH 07 06 05 04

The **McGraw-Hill** Companies

Contents

Contents (cont.)

Acknowledgments

Initial development of the *Kindergarten Everyday Mathematics* program was made possible by sustained support over several years from the Amoco Foundation, through the University of Chicago School Mathematics Project (UCSMP). Earlier projects supported by the National Science Foundation, the National Institute of Education, and the Benton Foundation provided us with insights into the often surprising capabilities of young children and the effectiveness of Minute Math exercises.

Feedback and advice from teachers willing to try revised versions of *Kindergarten Everyday Mathematics* were enormously helpful. There are too many such teachers to list, but their contributions are gratefully acknowledged.

Many UCSMP staff members and colleagues have been helpful to the authors, both in initial development of the program and in its various revisions.

Max Bell, Director
Elementary Materials Component
The University of Chicago School Mathematics Project

The *Kindergarten Everyday Mathematics* Viewpoint

We read exciting and informative stories, even great works of literature, to young children. We spontaneously communicate with them at their level of spoken and receptive language. It does not occur to us that we should limit our verbal interactions with young children because of their limited ability to use symbolic, written language.

Yet with mathematics, all too often, we treat learning as an entirely symbolic process. We fail to recognize and build upon children's rich and ever-expanding store of mathematical understanding and knowledge.

Kindergarten Everyday Mathematics remedies this situation, placing mathematics learning right in the midst of the varied, enjoyable, and understandable world where it rightfully belongs.

Kindergarten Everyday Mathematics is based on a philosophy, developed through research, about how young children learn mathematics. This research has shown that for most young children, it is appropriate to expand substantially their range of mathematics experiences and ideas. In addition to this expansion, *Kindergarten Everyday Mathematics* seeks to increase the time children spend on mathematics learning by integrating mathematics into other subject areas and by infusing mathematics into both the ongoing daily routines of the classroom and into those odd bits of time that occur during every school day.

Program Components

The *Kindergarten Everyday Mathematics* program provides children more than 100 hours of mathematics experiences. It is made up of the following components.

Program Guide and Masters (this book)

Program Guide

The first part of this book, the program guide, aims to familiarize you with the main features of *Kindergarten Everyday Mathematics* and its philosophy. You will probably find yourself rereading and referring to it often. It will help you understand how to use and adapt the program in ways that are consistent with its philosophy and yet tailored to work for you.

Activity Masters

Another part of this book contains blackline masters that you may want to reproduce for some of the activities in the *Teacher's Guide to Activities*. In this edition, these printed materials are also available as an optional individual consumable booklet, *Activity Sheets and Home Links*.

Home Link Masters

This book also contains a set of 44 masters for Home Link activities. Each Home Link suggests mathematics activities for family members and children to do together. Teachers can encourage families to use the Home Links by assuring them that these informal activities promote more real mathematics interest and growth for Kindergarten children than do pages of written arithmetic problems. Copies of these masters are intended to be sent home on roughly a weekly basis. Unless you wish to do so, you do not need to connect them to specific classroom activities. Home Links are also available in the consumable *Activity Sheets and Home Links*.

These and additional activities are available in *Mathematics at Home,* which you can purchase and send home, if you wish, instead of reproducing the Home Link masters. (See *Mathematics at Home* on page 3.)

Teacher's Guide to Activities

The *Teacher's Guide to Activities* is the heart of the program. Each activity in the guide is an educational task that involves the direct experience and participation of the child. The emphasis is on the learner, who is active, energetic, and directly engaged. This emphasis is central to the program's philosophy.

The activities are not necessarily used one per day. Some activities may fill the whole mathematics time or spill over into another day. Other activities are brief enough so that you may combine them with other activities. You may repeat any activity as often as the needs and responses of your children dictate. Always feel free to change the range of numbers in the activities so that they are appropriate for your class or for individual children.

Activities are designated for learning centers, the whole group, a small group, or partners. There are more activities than most teachers can use in a single school year, so make selections according to your own preferences and the needs of your children.

The authors have designated some important activities as "core" to help teachers of half-day programs or new teachers choose from among the activities. Core Activities are marked with bold type in the table of contents and with a "Core Activities" label on the pages where they appear.

Seven of the early activities in the *Teacher's Guide to Activities* are designated as "Ongoing Daily Routines." Please read about these in the Introduction section on page 3.

The table of contents at the front of the *Teacher's Guide to Activities* lists all activities in order. As you become familiar with the curriculum, you may wish to use them in a different order than they appear in the book. Some teachers spend more time on a particular strand by using activities that appear later in the *Teacher's Guide to Activities* to extend that strand. To facilitate that practice, there is a second table of contents, Activities by Strand, at the end of the book (beginning on page 299) that lists the activities by their mathematical strands.

Minute Math®

This important teacher resource consists of brief verbal interactions that provide support for the multiple exposure, spaced practice, and "problem solving" emphases of *Everyday Mathematics*. These activities are planned to be flexible, require no advance preparation or props, and can be accomplished in short small amounts of time anytime during the day. Children especially love the number stories when their own names and interests are used. (One class referred to the book as the "joke book.") Besides providing a variety of counting activities and much of the number story theme of the program, *Minute Math* provides reinforcement and review activities and gives children opportunities to think and talk about mathematics.

Content by Strand Poster

The Content by Strand Poster provides a comprehensive overview of how the mathematics strands and activities are interwoven throughout the school year. The reverse side of this poster lists all of the Guideposts by month as well as related Guideposts and Reminders pages in the *Teacher's Guide to Activities*.

Assessment Handbook (Kindergarten)

Assessment, at its best, helps reveal the development of each child's mathematical understanding, while giving you useful feedback about children's instructional needs. The *Assessment Handbook* is designed to provide helpful techniques for tracking the learning progress of children. It contains classroom-tested techniques used by Kindergarten teachers, with suggestions for observing children, keeping anecdotal records, and following their progress. It also provides ideas for encouraging children to reflect on and communicate about what they have learned.

It is important to respect the wide developmental range of children in any Kindergarten class—to think in terms of children's individual progress rather than to measure them against one another or against an arbitrary, rigid standard. Children need encouragement to try their best. Teachers and children must not always expect perfection but be willing to accept and learn from mistakes. It is imperative to reward effort, as well as performance, and to help children create works that are truly their own.

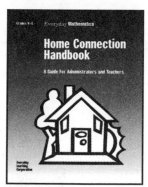

K–3 Teacher's Reference Manual

This reference book contains background with respect to the mathematics covered by activities in the *K–3 Everyday Mathematics* program. It consists of an introductory section focusing on the aims and philosophy of the program; followed by many brief, topical articles; and a comprehensive glossary of mathematical terms and of the particular pedagogic devices used in the K–3 program. If you are puzzled by some mathematical term, perhaps brought to you by a child or family members, a good place to start is the glossary. If you then want more information, you can proceed to one or more of the brief articles. A shorter glossary for teachers also appears in this program guide beginning on page 51.

Home Connection Handbook (K–6)

This handbook is a guide for teachers and administrators to help families become knowledgeable about the various features and benefits of *Everyday Mathematics*.

Mathematics at Home

If families want mathematics activities to do at home, in addition to or instead of the Home Links in the *Program Guide and Masters*, you may choose to purchase sets of *Mathematics at Home*. These three small, consumable booklets are printed in color and are for use at home by families. Book 1 can be sent home near the beginning of the school year, Book 2 perhaps in December, and Book 3 perhaps in March, about two-thirds of the way through the school year.

Program Structure

Multiple Exposures and Spaced Practice

People rarely master a new skill or idea the first time they experience it. For this reason, repeated exposure to key mathematical ideas over time is built into the Kindergarten program, usually in slightly different contexts for each new exposure. To be sure that children integrate new ideas into their learning experiences, the activities of each strand begin at a simple level and increase in complexity with children's experience. The interwoven design ensures that an activity is not "finished" the first time it is encountered but recurs periodically for further consideration and exploration.

Introduction to Kindergarten Mathematical Strands

The activities of the program are designed around eight mathematical content strands. Here are details about those eight strands:

1. Numeration

One of the goals of *Kindergarten Everyday Mathematics* is for children to be able to count, read, and write numbers past 100 by the end of Kindergarten. We recognize that children learn at different rates; thus, some will not meet this goal, and some will exceed it by the end of the school year. All children will make progress and increase in competence with oral counts, reading numbers, and writing number symbols to record counts and measures. Adjust the range of numbers within various activities according to the needs of your children. Maintain reasonably high expectations for all.

The Term *Digits*

When talking with children about numbers, begin to familiarize them with the term *digits,* which refers to the ten symbols, 0–9, that can be used to write all numbers. Once children become thoroughly accustomed to using the term *digits,* they will find the concept of place value much easier to understand. That is, children who think of 10, 17, and 52 as 2-digit numbers and 100, 320, and 512 as 3-digit numbers are ready to start thinking about the relative values of digits in different places within a multidigit number.

The Tricky Teens

Reading and writing the "teens" cause special problems for many children. Teaching children to hear the *four* in fourteen and the *six* in sixteen, for example, helps for some of the numbers. However, children must still memorize *eleven, twelve, thirteen,* and *fifteen*—numbers in which the "ones" place numbers are not so easily distinguished. Another problem is that the digit "one," which represents the number of tens, is written first, but referred to last (as in fourteen). The 2-digit numbers beyond the teens, such as *thirty-one* and *seventy-eight* have more consistent phonetic patterns. Try calling teens "the tricky teens." Tell children that all teen numbers have two digits and are written with the digit "1" first, meaning "10 and some more." For example, 17 is one ten and seven ones.

You can start an interesting discussion later in the year by asking your class whether 10, 11, and 12 are "teens" or not. If you have children who know how to count in languages other than English, you might discuss the fact that the same problems with "tricky" teens are found in many languages.

Physical action helps make these numbers more meaningful. For example, ask: *Can you eat a cracker in 12 (11, 15) bites? Can you jump 13 times?* Write the numbers on the chalkboard to help children associate the written symbols with the word names. When a teen number comes up in conversation, ask children how you should write it. Doing this often will help children be successful when it is their turn to write.

Rote Counting

Young children need to develop the ability to correctly sequence numbers through rote oral counting. Through repetition, they learn to hear, and later to see, the order and patterns in our number system.

▷ Counting on from a number other than 1 is the foundation for later activities with addition and subtraction. It becomes an efficient way to rote count to higher numbers.

▷ Counting backward may be difficult at first, but it will become easier with practice and familiarity. It helps children develop number sense.

▷ Skip counting (by 2s, 5s, and 10s) reveals some of the patterns in our number system. It is efficient and lays the foundation for multiplication. In counting by 2s (2, 4, 6, 8, ...), children will see and sense the even number pattern, as well as multiples of two.

Daily Counts throughout the Year

There are many ways to add variety to counting activities. Here are some ideas for playful counts. (Start at different and higher numbers as the year progresses.)

▷ Count and do "Noodle Knocks" (knock on head with knuckles).

▷ Count and nod your head; tap your foot, your knee, your stomach.

▷ Count and raise your arm.

▷ Count and clap.

▷ Count in whispers.

Also consider these more vigorous counts: jumping jacks, squat thrusts, sit-ups (keeping knees bent), toe touching, and so on. Remember that children also enjoy plain, rhythmic rote counting. Be sure to keep all oral counting sessions active, short, and lively. As the year progresses, include skip counting with and without calculators by 2s, 5s, and 10s, as well.

Tracking Counts with Calculators

Calculators in Kindergarten will rarely be used for doing arithmetic as such, but they are invaluable in displaying numerals and counts. It is easy to set up inexpensive calculators to "count" by 1s or "skip count" by 2s, 5s, and 10s (or any other number). Doing so is very useful because children can see the numbers that go with their verbal counts long before most of them can reliably and neatly write the numbers.

Rote Counting Guideposts

The stated year-end goal for oral counting is 115 and beyond. Counting past the barrier of 100 gives children a sense of the repetitive nature (and the comprehensibility!) of our number system.

Seven Guideposts are placed throughout the *Teacher's Guide to Activities* to remind you of the program's counting aims, and to keep children counting throughout the year. See pages 18–20 of this book for more information on Guideposts and program goals in general. Although many of the early counting activities suggest numbers from 0 to 10 and beyond, continue to use these counting activities with increasingly higher numbers throughout the year, varying the beginning numbers and extending the counting range.

Counting Things ("Rational Counting")

Young children also need to have many experiences counting things of various sizes, shapes, and arrangements. Through such experiences, children become increasingly adept at counting.

▷ Children learn to match one-to-one (one number name to one object) so that when given a specific number of objects to count, they end up with the same number each time.

▷ By counting 1, 2, 3, 4, 5, …, children are not simply matching names to objects; they're figuring out the number of objects in a whole group. (*Five* is not the name of the last object counted; *five* is the number of members in the group.)

▷ It is easier to count accurately (and to avoid counting some objects more than once), if the objects are arranged in a line or in rows rather than in irregular positions or are moved or marked as counted.

▷ Once children have mastered verbal counts by 5s and 10s, they can group and count large collections by those numbers quickly and more accurately.

▷ When materials, such as cups, treats, paper, pencils, crayons, coats, napkins, and manipulatives are being distributed, ask children: *How many* (or how much) *will we need? How can we find out?*

▷ Name or point to classroom objects and have children count them by touching them, collecting them, or counting them visually while remaining seated. Start with fewer and larger objects, such as tables and chairs. Later, as children's counting skills improve, use smaller, more numerous objects.

Once you are on the lookout for counting opportunities, you will be amazed at how often they occur. These everyday situations do much to help children appreciate mathematics as a useful and important tool.

Materials for Numeration Activities

RECOMMENDED

- ❏ calculators (solar-powered; ideally 1 per child)
- ❏ chalkboard or chart paper
- ❏ craft sticks (1,000) and rubber bands (valuable for grouping-by-10s activities)
- ❏ finger paints
- ❏ paper clips (12; 2")
- ❏ playing cards (about 4 decks)
- ❏ sand or water table or trays
- ❏ slates (1 per child, write-on/wipe-off boards or small chalk slates)
- ❏ teacher number cards (1–100, about 4" by 6", commercial or teacher-made)

VALUABLE

- ❏ counters other than pennies: (about 50 per child; poker chips, beads, buttons, beans, interlocking cubes, bear counters, and so on)
- ❏ file cards (3" by 5", at least 600)
- ❏ *How the Stars Fell into the Sky: A Navajo Legend* by Jerrie Oughton
- ❏ 100-bead counting frame
- ❏ *Number Bingo* game with 2-digit numbers (commercial or teacher-made)
- ❏ children's number cards from Activity Masters 3 and 4 (Children's Number Cards 0–7 and Children's Number Cards 8–15) in this book
- ❏ number line (commercial line –20 through 110, if you don't create a line with Number of the Day and Growing Number Line Routine, page 10, in the *Teacher's Guide to Activities*.)
- ❏ "stop" sign or red circle (helpful for interrupted counting activities)
- ❏ walk-on number line (0–20; commercial or teacher-made)

2. Measurement

The matching and comparing that children do naturally as they build with blocks, play store, dress dolls, and sift sand are necessary beginning steps toward understanding the measure units used for the main everyday types of measure: length, weight, volume or capacity, and elapsed time. Some activities involving matching and comparing are a necessary part of the introduction to the measurement with each of these units. Children often need help carrying out such comparisons carefully.

Many children come to Kindergarten able to use such measurement terms as years, pounds, inches, and miles. However, most children's ideas about the actual sizes of these units are quite vague. As they have more measuring experiences, they will begin to develop more accurate notions and will become more alert to measuring possibilities in both real-life situations and stories.

Measuring Activities

Some events lead naturally to measuring activities. For example, during the field-testing of this book, a child brought a gigantic candy bar to school to be shared with classmates. The class first wanted to know how much the candy bar weighed and used a kitchen scale to find out. Another child told the class that when her new baby sister was born, she weighed 7 lb 6 oz. The class then wanted to know how much that was, so they piled blocks, staplers, and other materials on the kitchen scale until it reached that weight. These items were collected in a bag, and children took turns "holding the baby."

Give children ample opportunities to weigh and measure themselves. Their own heights and weights are important to children. These measures give children personal standards against which they can compare weights of other animals and objects in their everyday lives. For example, when beavers were part of a classroom discussion during field testing, children were able to relate their own weights to that of a typical beaver.

Whenever possible, use objects that are currently of interest to children. They then experience measurement as a useful way to explore size and relative sizes, and the importance of using appropriate tools and units, while developing their understanding of the properties of objects. Cooking is an excellent measuring activity. Children learn to measure by measuring, especially in real-life situations.

Measuring Tools

Be alert for classroom activities in which children can help you prepare materials by measuring—using appropriate tools for length, weight, and capacity (volume). Many children have had little or no experience with the use of measuring instruments, and there are some pitfalls to watch out for. The most common errors are not lining up the 0-end of a ruler with one end of the object being measured, and being careless in making tight end-to-end arrangements of nonstandard length units. Remember to rotate the availability of measuring tools—bathroom scale, kitchen scale, rocker balance, measuring tapes, yardsticks/metersticks, and rulers—in the Math Center, so that children have many opportunities to use them for free exploratory play.

Measurement Units

Remind children to always designate units when they measure or count. Encourage them to say the words, such as "46 hands" instead of just "46." Some of the activities included in this program call for measuring with nonstandard units (such as children's own hands and feet). This is one way children can experience the need for units of a standard size.

Kindergarten Everyday Mathematics activities use both the U. S. customary system and the metric system. Only in the United States are customary system units still in common use. Science and industry in the United States, however, rely mainly on the metric system. Children need to be familiar with both systems. While the two different systems may seem confusing, adults are probably more confused than most children are.

Recording Measurements

Children can record the results of their measurement activities in a variety of ways. Initially, they may want to "draw" their results (for example, detailed pictures of a loaded rocker balance or lengths of centimeter cubes alongside objects being measured). Gradually, children may begin to include numbers and words (and symbols in some cases) to label their pictorial records. Recording, perhaps with your assistance, provides opportunities for numeration practice and allows for saving and comparing results for future reference.

Materials for Measurement Activities

RECOMMENDED

- ❏ centimeter cubes (500)
- ❏ containers of various shapes and sizes (empty, unbreakable)
- ❏ half-pint and pint milk cartons (empty) and filler material, such as sand, beans, or rice
- ❏ kitchen scale, 0–10 lb (or diet or cooking scale, 0–1 lb or 0–2 lb)
- ❏ kitchen timer, stopwatch, or clock with a second hand
- ❏ meter/yard cloth tape measures (marked in. and cm, preferably one for each pair of children)
- ❏ metersticks/yardsticks (10)
- ❏ people scale (bathroom type, preferably with lb and kg)
- ❏ rocker balance, preferably with transparent cups
- ❏ rulers (12", at least 12, ideally 1 per child)
- ❏ sand or water table or large trays

VALUABLE

- ❏ carpenter tapes (5, with in. and cm)
- ❏ growth chart for wall or door or mounted metersticks/yardsticks (preferably in both in. and cm)
- ❏ measuring cups and measuring spoons (standard, 3 or 4 sets of each)

3. Geometry

Young children come to school with an intuitive sense of their surroundings and with many informal ideas about geometric shapes. Many children are already familiar with the names of simple shapes (usually circles, squares, and triangles). The *Kindergarten Everyday Mathematics* program seeks to build on this prior knowledge and to prepare children for future analysis of the properties of and relationships among shapes. To accomplish this, children should have many and varied experiences with those shapes—playing, tracing, drawing, and constructing.

As always in this program, children have time to play and explore with materials before they use them in more structured activities. Materials should also remain available for explorations throughout the year. Free play with pattern blocks seems to be especially effective.

Once children can recognize plane figures as wholes, they can begin to analyze them. (What makes a triangle? A rectangle?) Later on, they can begin to think about such things as the relationships among different shapes and independence of size and shape. As children's vocabularies increase, so does their spatial awareness. However, with young children, this is not a formal process. They learn by hearing words used informally—the names of shapes, the names of geometric properties (sides, faces, corners), and relational words like *inside*, *outside*, *above*, and *below*. Encourage children to become aware of the geometric shapes all around us.

Materials for Geometry Activities

RECOMMENDED

- ❑ attribute blocks (1 class set)

- ❑ craft sticks (1,000)

- ❑ pattern blocks

- ❑ Pattern-Block Templates (at least 12)

- ❑ straws (small diameter) and twist-ties

VALUABLE

- ❑ pattern-block stickers

- ❑ two recordings by Hap Palmer, *Getting to Know Myself* and *Learning Basic Skills Through Music,* Vol. II (available as cassette tapes or CDs from Educational Activities, Inc., P.O. Box 87, Baldwin, NY 11510, 1-800-645-3739 or perhaps from educational catalogs or teacher supply stores)

4. Operations

Operations are the things we "do" to or with numbers. (*Everyday Teaching,* page 30) For two numbers, order relations express whether one is equal to, less than, or greater than the other. In *Kindergarten Everyday Mathematics,* the emphasis is on using operations and relations in solving concrete problems that arise from children's daily life in the classroom. Ask: *How many juice cups do we need on a day that someone is absent? How can we share snacks equally? Are there enough snacks for second helpings for everyone?*

Number Stories

The *Kindergarten Everyday Mathematics* approach to operations is to have children make up and act out their own number stories from the very beginning. This approach has the additional advantage of putting children in charge of their own learning and capitalizing on something they love—play acting. For a detailed description of the evolution of number stories and the introduction of symbolic language, see Number Stories throughout the Year, page 90, in the *Teacher's Guide to Activities*.

Reversibility of Operations

The approach of traditional mathematics programs has been to present children with addition first, then subtraction. The authors present addition and subtraction side by side as inverse operations, or "doing" and "undoing." This approach gives children a clearer understanding of the relationship between the two operations, and allows them to develop a wider range of strategies for solving problems later.

Relation Vocabulary

Make a conscious effort to use relation vocabulary—*bigger, smaller, more, less, the same, fewer, over, under, higher, lower, on the same level, equal,* and *equivalent.* Such vocabulary will increase children's abilities to perceive, use, and integrate these basic ideas into their own thinking.

Materials for Operations Activities

RECOMMENDED

- [ ] children's number cards from Activity Masters 3 and 4 (Children's Number Cards 0–7 and Children's Number Cards 8–15) in this book
- [ ] counters other than pennies (about 50 per child; poker chips, beads, buttons, beans, interlocking cubes, bear counters, and so on)
- [ ] craft sticks
- [ ] dominoes (5 or 6 sets; double–9)
- [ ] hardwood cubes (1", at least 50 to make a variety of cubes for games)
- [ ] rocker balance, preferably with transparent cups
- [ ] slates (1 per child; write-on/wipe-off boards or small chalk slates)

VALUABLE

- [ ] interlocking cubes
- [ ] walk-on number line (0–20; commercial or teacher-made)

5. Patterns and Functions

The unifying feature of the games and activities in the program that involve patterns, functions, and sequences is that they are all "rule-bound." Patterns are sets of elements that repeat in regular, predictable ways. Functions at the Kindergarten level are taught in a variety of "What's My Rule?" games. Later activities include an imaginary function machine that processes numbers according to a certain rule. A number (input) is put into the machine and transformed into a second number (output) by application of a specified rule. This device continues to be developed in future grade levels. Attribute activities involve sorting collections by "rules," for example, selecting a group of children by some property, such as those wearing something red. Sorting and categorizing various collections of things for storage, including classroom materials like blocks, manipulatives, and supplies are also a part of these activities. Sequences involve rules that determine the order of succession. Counts by 1s, 2s, 5s, 10s, and so forth, forward and back, are the beginning of more difficult sequences developed throughout the program.

Materials for Patterns and Functions Activities

RECOMMENDED

- ❏ attribute blocks (1 class set)
- ❏ chalkboard and chalk or chart paper and marker
- ❏ colored cubes, beads, or bear counters
- ❏ craft sticks
- ❏ hardwood cubes (1", at least 50 to make a variety of cubes for games)
- ❏ large paper or posterboard
- ❏ magazines
- ❏ paper clips (2"; 12; for spinners; inexpensive metal spinner arrows are commercially available)
- ❏ pattern blocks

VALUABLE

- ❏ cardboard pizza boards or other heavy-duty cardboard for looms
- ❏ pasta in different shapes and sizes (perhaps dyed different colors)
- ❏ straws (large diameter, plastic, drinking; 100)
- ❏ string (heavy-duty)
- ❏ yarn for weaving

6. Money

Money provides a natural link to the world of mathematics because most young children already recognize its importance in their everyday lives. Beginning in Kindergarten, money can be used as a fundamental tool for introducing children to ideas about place value, fractions, equivalence, and the decimal system.

Many young children have relatively few opportunities to use money in real-life situations. They need to play with coins in order to become familiar with their physical properties. As they learn to distinguish among coins, they can begin to assign values to them.

For Kindergarten children, there are some pitfalls in acquiring this knowledge. The names *nickel* and *dime*, for example, do not provide any clues as to the values of these coins. The sizes of the coins pose another problem: A nickel is bigger and thicker than a dime, but is only worth half as much; a dime is smaller and thinner than a penny, but is worth ten times as much. Children also need to explore the characteristics of $1 and $10 bills, which, along with coins, will become valuable means for building future mathematical concepts.

Kindergarten is a good place to start thinking about money. There is no doubt that interest and motivation are already high. The activities found in this book are playful and flexible. One of the main ingredients for success in using these activities is a good supply of real coins and realistic play bills in the classroom— as well as plenty of opportunities for children to play with them.

Incidental Use of Money

Children often come to class with small quantities of their own money. Use these occasions to help them identify and learn the values of their coins and their coin collections. This can be done in a large group or with individual children.

Collecting "milk money" or money for other purposes can also provide opportunities to sort, identify, and count money. You may want to display a record of money as it is collected. If so, use proper money notation. If children are collecting money for a common goal, a daily bar graph can make the activity more meaningful.

Using Money Materials

Real or play money is specified for many activities. However, whenever possible, use real money. In the case of pennies, nickels, and even dimes, real coins are as inexpensive or less expensive than play money, as well as more readily available. When dealing with quarters, half-dollars, dollars, and paper money, it is important to have at least a few samples of real money on hand. It is essential to have a large classroom supply of pennies (about 1,000 or $10.00 worth).

Pennies are the cheapest and best counters available. Since many households have jars full of surplus pennies, families are often willing to donate them without cost. The program materials list indicates some other coin quantities: about 10 nickels, 15 dimes, and 4 quarters per child. You may want to work with your principal, parent council, or individual families to help build a supply of real coins. Paper bills for play can be duplicated from Activity Masters 41–44 ($1 Bills; $1, $10, and $100 Bills).

You will need 1-inch wooden cubes to create the two kinds of money cubes used in some of the activities. You can write coin amounts directly on the cubes or on masking tape or self-stick dots. You can also glue coins to each side of a cube to make a money cube. You will need a sorting tray or muffin tin to serve as a money tray or "bank" and small magnifying glasses, at least one for each pair of children, for close observation of the coins (and other things in the classroom).

Materials for Money Activities
RECOMMENDED

- ❑ coins: pennies (1,000); nickels (10 per child); dimes (15 per child); quarters (4 per child)

- ❑ bills: $1, $10, $100 from Activity Masters 41–44, with real $1 and $10 bills to examine

- ❑ hardwood cubes (1", to be marked for money-game cubes and for use with other games)

- ❑ magnifying glasses (at least 1 for every 2 children)

- ❑ muffin tins, egg cartons, or other small bins for sorting

7. Clocks and Calendars

The concepts of telling time and measuring time duration within the framework of calendars and clocks are not easy for young children to grasp. Many children come to Kindergarten with bits and pieces of the whole: Many know their birth dates, their ages, and the times of their favorite television programs. They may refer to *days, weeks, years, hours, minutes,* and *seconds;* but their understanding of the duration of each of these units of measure is usually quite vague. This program includes many everyday activities that help children develop a sense of these concepts. There are activities in which children keep track of time on the calendar, the clock, and the Growing Number Line. There are games and activities that help them develop a sense of sequential order (making simple timelines, for example) as well as many timed activities to help them develop a sense of duration. In addition to the specific "time" activities described in this book, be on the lookout for natural opportunities to incorporate time concepts as they arise in your classroom. For example, help children track their own physical and intellectual growth over time.

Time is often a factor in science: "How long will it take for the snow to melt? The marble to roll down the block ramp?" "Countdowns," such as "How many weeks until vacation? Days to a class celebration? Minutes until recess? Seconds to line up?," demonstrate logical choices of time units. If you include recording as part of these activities, children will get much practice reading and writing numbers with two or more digits.

Use ordering vocabulary, such as *before, after, late,* and *morning*. Include such clock and calendar references as: *We'll have 20 minutes for recess.* Or: *We'll have a surprise tomorrow.* When you check the clock, periodically model what you are doing and include children in the process: *We need to be at gym just before 11. Help me check the hour hand. Are we early? Late?* Or: *Lunch ends at half past 12. Tell me when the hour hand is just about halfway between the 12 and the 1.* References such as these will help familiarize children with the language and the concepts of time while avoiding premature instruction in the intricacies of accurate reading of clocks.

Materials for Clocks and Calendars Activities

RECOMMENDED

- ❑ brads
- ❑ clock face with movable hands for the classroom door
- ❑ daily classroom calendar
- ❑ demonstration clock
- ❑ drum or metronome
- ❑ kitchen timer
- ❑ wall clock (preferably with a sweep-second hand)

VALUABLE

- ❑ clock face stamps
- ❑ *Learning Basic Skills Through Music,* Vol. II by Hap Palmer
- ❑ *The Tortoise and the Hare* storybook (many sources)

8. Data and Chance

Collecting, organizing, and presenting data in tables and graphs have become increasingly important in our complex world. Even young children can participate in gathering information, displaying it, and making counts and comparisons.

The process always begins with a question. For Kindergarten children, the most meaningful questions are those connected with real problems in the classroom and with collecting information that directly concerns them.

The other components in all graphing activities are collecting data, displaying them, and discussing and explaining the results. In these beginning experiences, the first and second steps often go hand in hand—data accumulate as the graph or other display is being made.

Generating Data with Surveys

As the year goes on, children can conduct "surveys" to generate data. They may think of a question that they want every class member to answer such as: *Are you afraid of the dark?* They record each child's response on a class list, "writing" responses as best they can. You can assist children in graphing the results individually or as a class. Survey taking is a motivating and satisfying independent activity for many Kindergartners.

Graphing Activities

The graphing activities that are repeated throughout this program involve answering the question "How many?" (How many birthdays, pets, and so on).

Most of the activities are best displayed using some kind of bar graph. These might be made more concrete by piling up blocks or accumulating small pictures or squares of paper into bars. Eventually, you may just want to color squares to make bars on grid paper. Make an effort to see that children become familiar with both vertical and horizontal bar graphs. Finished graphs should always include labeled axes, perhaps arrived at by class discussion. In addition to the activities in the data and chance strand, there are many activities in other strands that lend themselves to interesting data-collecting and graphing possibilities.

Discussion of Graphs

When leading a discussion about a finished graph, try an open-ended question, such as: *What did we find out?* before asking specific questions. Eliciting ideas for a title for a graph can also lead to a lively discussion. Read and interpret graphs with the class. You and the children can ask many questions about graphs, such as: *Which had the most responses? The least? How many more said 'Yes' than said 'No'? How many responses altogether?* One advantage of graphs made with objects or slips of paper is that children can touch and manipulate the graph as they try to understand it and figure out answers to the above questions.

Materials for Data and Chance Activities
RECOMMENDED

- ❏ dice
- ❏ posterboard or tagboard
- ❏ meterstick/yardstick
- ❏ small stick-on note pads

Some Pervasive Elements of the Program

Problem Solving

In most school basal texts, and for many teachers, problem solving is almost exclusively linked to "story problems." *Kindergarten Everyday Mathematics* does suggest working on number stories, and many flexible examples are given in *Minute Math.* But, as in *K–6 Everyday Mathematics* more generally, the program sets up a problem-rich environment so problem situations arise in all strand activities. Read the Problem Solving essay in the *K–3 Teacher's Reference Manual* for more detail.

Estimation Skills and Number Sense

Being able to make educated guesses about counts or measures is a powerful tool. Throughout *Everyday Mathematics,* estimating is encouraged in a variety of situations. Young children need help distinguishing between a wild guess and a "ballpark" figure: *We have only 30 children in the class and not all of them drink milk, so how could we have a million milk cartons?* Children love to make guesses and then verify how close they have come. Opportunities to estimate occur naturally during the course of the the school day. Ask: *About how many steps to the door? About how many cartons of milk do we drink in a day? In a week?*

You can also set up estimation activities. Create an Estimation Station in the classroom consisting of a jar that can be loaded with varying amounts of different items, a set of blank file cards on which to write estimates, and a collection box for the written estimates. It is helpful to have a reference jar the same size and shape as the one at the station with a known quantity of selected items. Change the contents of the Estimation Station jar frequently. Recording estimates provides valuable number-writing practice. Checking the actual amount of the jar's contents and then comparing this amount to children's estimates provides excellent counting, measuring, numeration, and graphing opportunities. Counting can be done by 1s, 2s, 5s, or 10s. The more opportunities children have to estimate, the more accurate they become. They become more comfortable taking risks, too. In real life, it is often useful and important to be able to look at a problem and reach an approximate answer before trying to figure out an exact answer.

Communication

Throughout all the mathematical strands of the program, it is important to encourage children to discuss and share their thoughts, make connections among ideas and experiences, and use their powers of reasoning and insight to solve problems. You can do this by creating a nonthreatening environment where children feel comfortable sharing their ideas with others. You can encourage dialogue by asking such questions as: *Tell us how you thought of that? Why do you think so?*

Labels and Units

Labels and units are important for every count and measure. Children learn to consider the units being used when they are manipulating numbers—not just "ten" but "10 what?"—cats, people, erasers, and so on. In the everyday world, numbers almost never appear without some label, unit, or context.

Reversibility of Most Actions

Children become accustomed to the reversibility of most actions: put in, take out; add, subtract; put together, take apart; leave, return; expand, shrink; spend, earn; and many others. They become aware, too, of the uses of patterns and rules. As the language of mathematics becomes familiar to them, children begin to feel at ease in the mathematics domain.

Calculators

By the time children have reached Kindergarten, most of them will have observed other people using calculators. Many children will even have used calculators themselves. Calculators are part of the everyday world, and this makes them interesting and exciting for young children. At the Kindergarten level, children seldom use calculators for operations on numbers. However, calculators do allow children to display and read numbers long before they have the physical skills to write them. It is easy to set up a calculator to count by 1s, 2s, 5s, 10s, or other numbers, both forward and backward, thus enabling children to produce and read these numbers before they develop writing skills. On occasion as the year progresses, children can use calculators to solve interesting, everyday numerical problems that arise in the classroom, including cumulative scores, large counts, and "how many more" kinds of questions. Calculators are, therefore, an integral part of *Kindergarten Everyday Mathematics*.

Using the Program

Half-Day vs. Full-Day Kindergarten Programs

The *Everyday Mathematics* authors believe that each of the activities in the *Teacher's Guide to Activities* has value and interest. However, relatively few teachers, particularly those involved in half-day programs, should try to use them all. You can construct a solid half-day or full-day program from the following elements:

▷ Daily Routines are essential to the program. They ensure that children have mathematics experiences every day, and they provide a structure within which children's growing mathematics concepts and skills can flourish. They are described at the beginning and are among the first activities in the *Teacher's Guide to Activities*. As one teacher put it, "They are a crucial and defining feature of the program."

▷ Core Activities (including the "Ongoing Daily Routines") provide experiences with the most essential features of the program. Those activities are clearly marked as "Core Activities" in the table of contents, the Activities by Strand section, and on individual activities in the *Teacher's Guide to Activities*. Make every effort to incorporate at least these activities into your Kindergarten instructional plan—whether you teach in a half-day or a full-day program.

▷ *Minute Math* fits well into a program where time is in short supply. (See page 2 of this program guide for a description of this component.)

Before the First Day

Here are things you will need to do before the first day of school:

▷ Read and become familiar with this *Program Guide and Masters* and all other components of the program.

▷ Read the Before the First Day section in the *Teacher's Guide to Activities* for details of tasks that are best accomplished before children arrive.

Guideposts and Reminders

The dictionary defines *guidepost* as "a sign for the guidance of travelers." In this case, the travelers are children making a journey toward mathematical awareness and understanding, guided by you, their teacher. Keep in mind that the travelers may not all move at the same speed; the most important aspect of their journey is that they are making progress.

Since plain and fancy verbal counting abilities are one important foundation for arithmetic, counting activities appear in many places in *Kindergarten Everyday Mathematics*. To help you keep track of progress throughout the year, seven "Guideposts and Reminders" are spaced among the activities. Besides the guideposts for counting and progress in other skill areas, these pages contain reminders, suggestions, and notes intended to help you—especially those of you who are new to *Kindergarten Everyday Mathematics*.

Year-End Learning Goals

Our research on the actual capabilities of Kindergarten children from a wide range of schools showed that more than 80 percent of beginning Kindergarten children could already count 14 dots on a card, and many could count orally well beyond that. We also found, for example, that at the beginning of Kindergarten, about 30 percent could read and write the number "57," about 40 percent could read and write the number "100," and 40 percent could count backward from 10. At the end of that Kindergarten year, about 90 percent of the children could correctly share 12 things among 3 people, and 60 percent could respond correctly to "Please give me half of these 12 blocks." Yet in many schoolbooks, numbers beyond 20, division, and fractions are deferred until well beyond Kindergarten. It surely seems that what many children learn without the help of school instruction, many more could learn with excellent experience and instruction.

Based on findings such as these and our teaching experience, we set goals that are optimistic about children's capabilities and willingness to learn. We then tried to find and invent playful activities that would help children achieve those outcomes. In the variety of schools where we work, children have responded wonderfully to those activities and the expectations built into them.

Here are suggested year-end goals built into *Kindergarten Everyday Mathematics*. Suggestions for assessment are found in the *Kindergarten Assessment Handbook*.

▷ Verbally counts 20 or more objects in a random arrangement.

▷ Performs interrupted verbal counting beyond 100.

▷ Counts backward from 22 or higher.

▷ Counts by 2s beyond 30.

▷ Counts by 5s beyond 110.

▷ Counts by 10s beyond 110.

▷ Reads any number, 100 or less.

▷ Writes any number, 100 or less.

▷ Understands basic meanings of addition and subtraction in real situations, in children's own number stories, in oral problems, with concrete objects, and on number lines. These concepts are generally assessed with oral rather than written exercises.

▷ Understands 2-digit numbers in terms of 10s and 1s.

▷ Understands equivalent expressions as two or more different expressions of the same number, perhaps by acting out a variety of ways of expressing the same (small) number. (For example, 6 is the same as, or equivalent to, 2 + 4, 5 + 1, 7 − 1, ...)

▷ Recognizes many non computational uses of numbers through daily experiences. Example: Counts snacks, children, or days until a special event; measures length, weight, elapsed time, or cost; and has experience with certain reference frames such as clocks, calendars, temperatures, or ordinal numbers.

▷ Estimates comfortably, using such language as *about how many, about how much,* or *about what cost.*

▷ Identifies and uses measuring tools for linear, weight, and volume measures.

▷ Performs simple data collection and graphing.

▷ Has experience with basic geometry shapes and symmetry concepts; recognizes and names basic plane and solid figures.

▷ Knows the value of a penny, nickel, and dime; recognizes a quarter.

▷ Estimates time on an analog clock using only the hour hand.

Ongoing Assessment

Certain activities include "ongoing assessment" as part of their focus. These activities present convenient opportunities for you to observe and record children's progress while they are actively engaged in the activities. See the *Assessment Handbook* for more details about ongoing and more formal, periodic assessment.

Notes about the Word *Center*

When an activity in the *Teacher's Guide to Activities* is labeled "Center," it refers to your Math Center. This is a special area or shelf in the classroom where you keep a variety of mathematics materials so that children have easy access to them. If you already have learning centers in your classroom, you probably have a Math Center that fits this description. If you do not have one, it would be useful to create a "home-base" area for mathematics materials and activities. Center suggestions are intended to be adaptable to individual differences in classroom schedule, organization, and style.

The Math Center promotes a wide variety of uses. In more structured settings, individuals or small groups can explore an activity that you want everyone to try but do not want to do with the whole class. (The activity may be hard to manage with the whole group, materials may be limited, or you may want to work more closely with one or a few children, as in an assessment.) The Math Center works well for structured experiences in which children try an activity and then bring their results, observations, and questions back to share with the whole group, collect data for a class graph, or make a page for a number storybook.

Less structured uses of the Math Center include free play. Many teachers have found it valuable to occasionally have a distinct Math Center time during which children limit their choices for free play to this area. When children concentrate their time and attention on pattern blocks, scales, measures, geometry templates, selected games, and other mathematics-related materials, highly imaginative and complex designs and play can evolve.

The Math Center should be available to children during any free-choice time of the day. Children need opportunities to explore materials that they will use in future learning activities. Free exploration promotes the sort of familiarity that will help children when they use these materials in guided and extended ways. In addition, children often need and want to continue to play with materials they have used during a structured activity. Also, it can be revealing to observe what materials children select on their own and how they use them.

Finally, you should always encourage children to use tools, such as calculators, rulers, balances, scales, manipulatives for counting or measuring, and number cards, from the Math Center, whenever they need them. For example, they may want to measure a block building, play "store," write a phone number, or weigh a seashell. It is through this kind of integration of mathematics with everyday classroom life that children develop a true understanding of the usefulness of mathematics.

Games

Games are an important part of *Kindergarten Everyday Mathematics*. They allow children to discover ideas and to develop an understanding of mathematics concepts at their own pace. They provide opportunities for the playful practice of mathematics skills and serve as an enjoyable alternative to tedious drills and worksheets. Games also put children in a position to learn from and teach one another as they play.

Children use games for different purposes. Some children may want or need to play a particular game over and over again to reinforce a concept, build speed or confidence, or simply enjoy themselves. The games included in the program provide excellent tools for individualizing instruction while continuing to emphasize cooperative group work. Numbers or concepts can usually be varied within a game to make it easier or more difficult or to emphasize different skills. For example, children can play *Top-It* and most of the other card games with larger or smaller numbers in the card deck to adjust the level of difficulty. You can add a recording aspect to *Digits Game* to emphasize numeration. Children can play *Monster Squeeze* with higher numbers, with or without a number line.

Many teachers are justifiably concerned about the competitive aspect associated with most games and the impact of competition on both individual children and on classroom life. Teachers are also concerned that "losing" a game may intimidate some children, especially those less experienced with games who don't realize that "winning" most games depends more on chance than skill. Others note that competitive games may be inconsistent with teaching philosophies that emphasize cooperation and individual progress rather than competition among children.

The authors respect these views. Teachers have suggested several ways to de-emphasize competition as you make games a part of your mathematics program. For example, many children have already learned the ideas of winning and losing from family and friends. Explain to children that in your classroom, you do not want to have winners and losers in games, even though children might have them when they play games in other places. Teachers involve children in making a list of possible reasons for not having "winners" and "losers" in the classroom, such as "We should help each other play and learn"; "Losing sometimes makes people feel sad"; "Games should be fun and interesting to everyone."

Kindergarten is an important year for shaping children's attitudes toward game playing. Ideally, Kindergarten children will *play to see what happens, not to see who wins*. In talking with children about games, focus on what occurred during the game—*Was it fun? Interesting? Easy? Difficult? Long? Short?* In many cases, game descriptions do not need to include a designation of winners and losers. For example, instructions for *Top-It* specify that play ends when children have used up all the cards. Even in games where children do complete play by accumulating points, it is not necessary to label the person who has the most points the winner. You can teach a useful lesson in probability by flipping a coin to decide (before or after playing) if the person with the fewest points or the most points "wins." You can encourage children to keep a record of their own scores before putting the game away or playing again.

Many of the games in *Kindergarten Everyday Mathematics* will be unfamiliar to children's families. Consider the benefits of signing-out games for home use: Children practice mathematics skills at home, families learn about the program, children learn to be responsible for materials, and children can teach their families—an empowering experience for them. You can follow a procedure similar to the one used by a library. Put materials for games in a large envelope or plastic bag, along with an instruction sheet. You might also include a sheet for children and families to write comments about the game, perhaps arranging for families to read one another's comments. Sometimes families suggest interesting game variations in those comments. Establish a policy about when games should be returned. A shorter borrowing period increases the chances of return without loss of materials. One night is generally sufficient.

Slates

Slates provide convenient and inexpensive surfaces on which children can write their mathematical work. They provide an excellent way to assess individual responses. Children may write on the write-on/wipe-off boards suggested in the materials list with special pens or crayons. Small, individual chalkboards are also excellent. Establish a regular routine for the distribution and pickup of slates in your classroom. Have children get into the habit of cleaning their slates at the end of each activity. Children can use a sock to wipe the slates, as well as to keep the chalk (or a write-on crayon or pen) together. Encourage children to use their slates to practice number writing during free-play time. The classroom chalkboard also provides a good place to work with individuals, small groups, or the whole class.

Classroom Materials and Supplies

Kindergarten Everyday Mathematics requires an investment in manipulative materials and supplies. Most of the following are available from school supply companies. You may find that many of these materials are already a part of your classroom.

RECOMMENDED FOR THE PROGRAM

- ❏ attribute blocks (1 class set)
- ❏ bills: $1, $10, $100 from Activity Masters 41–44, with real $1 and $10 bills to examine
- ❏ brads
- ❏ calculators (solar-powered; ideally 1 per child)
- ❏ centimeter cubes (500)
- ❏ chalkboard or chart paper
- ❏ children's number cards from Activity Masters 3 and 4 (Children's Number Cards 0–7 and Children's Number Cards 8–15) in this book
- ❏ clock face with movable hands for the classroom door
- ❏ coins: pennies (1,000); nickels (10 per child); dimes (15 per child); quarters (4 per child)
- ❏ containers of various shapes and sizes (empty, unbreakable)
- ❏ craft sticks (1,000) and rubber bands
- ❏ daily classroom calendar (See Building the Monthly Calendar Routine, page 30 in the *Teacher's Guide to Activities*.)
- ❏ demonstration clock for classroom
- ❏ dice ($\frac{5}{8}$"; 1 pair for every 2 children)
- ❏ dominoes (double-9; 5 or 6 sets)
- ❏ finger paints
- ❏ half-pint and pint milk cartons (empty) and filling materials such as sand, beans, or rice
- ❏ hardwood cubes (1", at least 50 to make a variety of cubes for games)
- ❏ kitchen scale (0–10 lb)
- ❏ kitchen timer, stopwatch, or clock with second hand
- ❏ magnifying glasses (small, plastic; at least 1 for every 2 children)
- ❏ meter/yard cloth tape measures (marked in both in. and cm; 1 for each pair of children)
- ❏ metersticks/yardsticks (10)
- ❏ muffin tins, egg cartons, or other small bins for sorting

- ❏ outdoor thermometer (preferably with both Fahrenheit and Celsius scales)

- ❏ paper clips (2";12; for spinners; inexpensive metal spinner arrows are commercially available)

- ❏ Pattern-Block Templates (at least 12)

- ❏ pattern blocks (at least 1 set for each classroom)

- ❏ people scale (bathroom type, preferably with both lb and Kg markings)

- ❏ playing cards (about 4 decks; these can be made using 3" by 5" file cards or blank playing cards) (See Classroom Playing Cards, page 169, in the *Teacher's Guide to Activities.*)

- ❏ posterboard or tagboard

- ❏ rocker balance, preferably with transparent cups

- ❏ rulers (12"; at least 12, ideally 1 per child)

- ❏ sand or water table or trays

- ❏ slates (1 per child; write-on/wipe-off boards or small chalk slates)

- ❏ straws (small diameter, plastic, drinking; box of 500) and twist-ties (box of 2,000), (for constructing geometric figures, often inexpensively available at party-supply stores)

- ❏ teacher number cards (1–100, about 4" by 6", commercial or teacher-made)

- ❏ wall clock (preferably with a sweep-second hand)

VALUABLE ADDITIONS TO THE PROGRAM

- ❏ base-10 blocks (or occasionally borrow from first grade teacher for exploratory play)

- ❏ blank playing cards (4 decks)

- ❏ cardboard pizza boards or other heavy-duty cardboard

- ❏ carpenter tapes (5, with in. and cm markings)

- ❏ clock face stamps

- ❏ counters other than pennies (about 50 per child; poker chips, beads, buttons, beans, interlocking cubes, bean counters, and so on)

- ❏ Cuisenaire® rods (about 4 sets for exploratory play)

- ❏ diet or cooking scale (capacity to about 1 lb (500 gm) or 2 lbs (1 kg))

- ❏ drum or metronome

- ❏ "feely" bag (an opaque bag or sack) or "feely" box (made by cutting a hole in any box with a top)

- ❏ file cards (3" by 5", at least 600)

- growth chart for wall or door, or mounted metersticks/yardsticks (preferably in both in. and cm)
- interlocking cubes
- lightweight rope or cord (about 20 feet)
- measuring cups and measuring spoons (standard, 3 or 4 sets of each)
- *Number Bingo* game with 2-digit numerals (commercial or teacher-made)
- number line (commercial number line –20 through 110, if you don't create a line with Number of the Day and Growing Number Line Routine, page 10, in the *Teacher's Guide to Activities*.)
- 100-bead counting frame
- old magazines
- pasta in different shapes and sizes (perhaps dyed different colors)
- pattern-block stickers
- small stick-on note pads
- stick-on paper dots (1-inch or $\frac{1}{2}$-inch diameter)
- "stop" sign or red circle (helpful for interrupted counting activities)
- straws (large diameter, plastic, drinking; 100) (for weaving; also available at party-supply stores)
- string (heavy-duty)
- walk-on number line (0–20; commercial or teacher-made)
- yarn for weaving

BOOKS, TAPES, OR CDs REFERRED TO IN ACTIVITIES

- *Getting to Know Myself,* Hap Palmer (Educational Activities, Inc., P.O. Box 87, Baldwin, NY, 11510. Telephone 1-800-645-3739, Web site www.edact.com. CD or cassette)
- *How Big Is a Foot?,* Rolf Myller (Dell Publishing, 1991)
- *How the Stars Fell into the Sky: A Navajo Legend,* Jerrie Oughton (Houghton Mifflin, 1992)
- *Learning Basic Skills through Music,* Vol. II. Hap Palmer (See above)
- *The Tortoise and the Hare* storybook (many sources)

MISCELLANEOUS

- ❏ baking supplies (bowls, cookie sheets, mixing spoons)
- ❏ beanbags
- ❏ checkerboards and checkers
- ❏ cotton swabs
- ❏ dress-up clothes
- ❏ fabric scraps
- ❏ frozen juice cans
- ❏ maps (a variety of city, state, U.S., world)
- ❏ masking tape
- ❏ round paper doilies
- ❏ sandpaper
- ❏ small food items (crackers, grapes, raisins)
- ❏ sorting materials (buttons, shells, bottle caps, beads, macaroni)
- ❏ sponges (small) or vegetables for printing shapes
- ❏ spring-clip clothespins (1 package)
- ❏ wallpaper samples

Home and School Communication

Discussion, experimentation, and play are at the heart of *Kindergarten Everyday Mathematics*. Family members who have been accustomed to conventional mathematics programs may think that because children are not bringing home daily or weekly arithmetic sheets, they are not learning or doing mathematics. These assumptions may not change easily. It is important to help families understand the concepts that underlie this program and to value the range of its mathematical content so that they can become partners in their children's learning.

The *Home Connection Handbook* included in the *Kindergarten Everyday Mathematics* teacher's package, has many general suggestions for creating strong links to families throughout the K–6 years.

Home Links

These sheets suggest activities for family members and children to do together. They are discussed in detail on page 2. You can find Home Link masters in this book beginning on page 107. Alternatives to the masters are the consumable *Activity Sheets and Home Links* or the three consumable booklets, *Mathematics at Home*. See page 3 for more information about *Mathematics at Home*.

Letters Home

Letters are an effective way to communicate with families. A sample introductory letter and suggestions for additional letters are in the Appendices section of this program guide.

Open Houses and Conferences

To help families feel valued and understand and appreciate their children's mathematics program, invite them to come to the classroom to experience mathematics activities for themselves.

Many of the activities and materials in the *Teacher's Guide to Activities* lend themselves to family explorations. If you plan to include children in an open house, the activities may be adapted so that adults and children can work together. A list of suggestions follows.

Suggestions for Mathematics Open House Activities (whole group)

▷ Daily Routines: Attendance Sign-In, Job Chart, Temperature, Calendar, Number of the Day, Cleanup Count

▷ *Monster Squeeze:* using a number line; "mental math" activity

▷ "What's My Rule?"

Suggestions for Mathematics Open House Activities (individuals, partners, and small groups):

▷ Pattern Blocks: Introduce free play; also include cards with questions, such as: *How many ways can you cover a trapezoid? A rhombus (diamond)? A hexagon?*

▷ Body Measures: Family members can trace one of their own feet, cut out the tracing and then use it to measure the rug, a table, or an object—then remeasure using a standard ruler.

▷ Things That Sink or Float

▷ Modeling-Dough Numbers

▷ Favorite Color Graph: Each parent can choose from a pile of precut colored squares of paper and put his or her choice on a prepared tagboard. Lead a discussion on what the graph shows.

▷ Patterns with Craft Sticks: free play

▷ *Disappearing Train*

▷ Card games (*Top-It*)

▷ Symmetry: art projects

▷ *Raft Game*

▷ Geoboards

▷ *Probability Game* (Graphing Sums of Dice Throws)

▷ Straw and Twist-Tie Constructions

▷ Counting on Calculators

Additional Home Activities

Here are some additional brief activities tailored to Kindergarten children that you might suggest to families, perhaps in letters home or at open houses and conferences.

For Children's Individual Activities

▷ Find how many bites it takes to eat an apple, a cookie, and so on.

▷ Find how many things at home are shaped like a square, circle, triangle, and so on.

▷ Find how many people have a foot that is a standard foot long.

▷ Tell which numbers you use on your television dial.

▷ Find how many shoes are in your (or anyone else's) closet.

▷ Find how many stairs are in your house.

▷ Find how many floors are in your house or apartment building.

▷ Find how many rooms are in your house or apartment.

▷ Find how many socks are in your sock drawer.

▷ Find how many pairs of socks are in your sock drawer.

▷ Find how many books are on your bookshelf.

▷ Find how many timepieces (clocks, timers, calendars, and so on) are in your home.

▷ Find how many measuring tools (rulers, yardsticks, scales, and so on) are in your home.

▷ Find how many standard feet (on a ruler) there are across your bedroom.

▷ Find how many of your own feet it takes to cross your bedroom (heel to toe).

For Activities Shared with Family Members, Friends, and Relatives

▷ Make a simple recipe, with the child measuring.

▷ Encourage children to do such tasks as these:

- Set the table, counting out places, flatware, plates, napkins, and cups.

- Sort the silverware drawer.

- Sort and fold socks.

- Sort small change.

- Sort buttons, craft materials, family photos, and other interesting objects.

▷ Count anything, such as coins, stairs, colors, or cars on a freight train.

▷ Read numerals on houses and elevators.

▷ Read price tags while grocery shopping.

▷ Talk about numbers on the phone, TV, clocks, and so on.

▷ Weigh family members.

▷ Weigh meats, vegetables, packages, and cans.

▷ Measure for various purposes, such as hanging pictures, sewing, or making a birdhouse.

Appendices

Ideas for Letters Home

Introduction to *Kindergarten Everyday Mathematics*

This year, your child will be using *Kindergarten Everyday Mathematics,* a program created through the University of Chicago School Mathematics Project. This program is based on research and experience that show young children are capable of far more mathematics learning in Kindergarten than was previously believed possible, provided that the content is presented in ways appropriate for children of Kindergarten age.

To many of us who learned to think of mathematics primarily as written work, it may be hard at first to believe that considerable mathematics learning is taking place in this program. Few papers come home. The children seem to be playing! However, these playful activities are meaningful and productive and help children become independent and comfortable thinkers about mathematical ideas. Research has shown that young children often have difficulty with written and symbolic mathematics if it is emphasized too early—before a strong foundation based on experience and understanding has been built.

You will see your child become excited by a wealth of mathematics activities, including counting, numeration, measurement, geometry, patterns, data collecting, and calculator use. Classroom routines give children real-life opportunities to develop and refine a variety of mathematics skills. These include such activities as keeping track of the days of school on a number line, monitoring and graphing daily temperature and other weather conditions, recording attendance, counting the time it takes to cleanup, and charting the daily schedule.

We hope that through *Kindergarten Everyday Mathematics,* both you and your child will find that mathematics is useful, enjoyable, varied, and meaningful. Just as we know that telling stories and reading books to children help to foster a love of reading, your support of mathematics learning will help your child develop lasting confidence and competence. These will carry over into many areas in everyday life and the school curriculum, this year and in the years to come.

Your comments and questions are always most welcome.

More Suggestions for Letters Home

In your letters home to families, be sure to keep them informed about the mathematics activities taking place in your classroom. Following are excerpts from letters written by some *Kindergarten Everyday Mathematics* teachers. Feel free to modify these or to use them as models.

Thanksgiving Collection

The children are very proud of the number of cans of food we have collected for the food drive, thanks to all of you. A favorite activity has been counting all these cans—70 so far—and recording the numbers on a grid. We have counted the cans from 1, counted on from the last recorded number, added to the last recorded number, arranged the cans in rows of 10, and counted them by 10s. Now we are weighing them and finding the total number of pounds on a calculator.

Number Books

Our number books will be coming home soon. When you look at them with your child, it may be helpful to know a little about what went into making them.

The focus was not on the artistic merit of the children's pictures but on the clarity of the counts. Our standard for the counts is that the child be able to count the number of elements in the picture—and count the same way each time.

Number Stories throughout the Year

In telling number stories, children are beginning to learn strategies for solving addition and subtraction problems and are becoming acquainted with the appropriate symbolic language.

Children sometimes roll dice for their starting numbers. As they count the number of dots on the cubes, they begin to get mental pictures of what a "five" or a "six," etc. looks like. If they roll a "two" and are telling a "seven story," they have to decide whether to add or subtract—and by how much. A few children have instant answers, but most need counters to help them. Ask your child to tell you a six story, a ten story, or a zero story.

The 100 Day

Coming up very soon, on (your date), is the 100th day of school—cause for a major celebration! One of the things we will be doing in our classroom is building a "100 Museum," containing a collection of 100 things brought in by each child. When we first mentioned this museum to the children, there was general enthusiasm and a few worries ("My family doesn't have 100 things at home." "How can I carry 100 things to school?"). We are hoping that by 100 Day, 100 will be a friendly number to all the children.

In our discussions, children have been coming up with ideas about what they plan to bring in (100 dinosaurs, 100 hats, 100 paper clips, 100 baseball cards). We have been talking about ways to count out their collections so that the children don't lose track of the numbers (making ten groups of ten objects each, for example).

We always welcome parental involvement, and your support of this project will be most appreciated. Remember, though, that the more children are able to do themselves in assembling and counting out their collections, the more they will learn, and the prouder they will be. We have been encouraging children not to wait until The Day to bring in their collections. We need time to count, weigh, and admire the displays as 100 Day draws near.

Graphing Sums of Dice Throws

The latest craze in our classroom has been graphing dice throws. A discussion erupted as we handed out the numbered grids and someone said, "There's no 1!" It didn't take long for our young mathematicians to figure out that there can't be a number 1 when throwing two cubes (which have at least one dot on each).

To graph the throws, a child rolls two cubes, figures out the total, and marks the square in the appropriate column by either writing the number (or number combination) in the square or by coloring the square in. Each child continues until one number "wins" (one column is filled). We took a master grid, recorded the winning numbers on it, and then talked about why 6, 7, and 8 did so much better than the other numbers. Your children are beginning to explore probability theory.

Weaving

The children are becoming expert weavers as they complete headbands, belts, rugs, and pillows. Weaving is actually part of our mathematics curriculum and provides children with excellent experiences with patterning. It also helps children develop spatial orientation, along with such orientation words as *over* and *under, in* and *out, back* and *forth*. Of course, it also teaches children to be patient and to persevere.

Additional Songs, Poems, and Chants for the Classroom

FIVE LITTLE DUCKS

Five little ducks went out to play,

Over the hill and far away.

When mother duck went *quack, quack, quack,*

Four little ducks came waddling back.

When mother duck went *quack, quack, quack,*

Four little ducks came waddling back.

(Repeat with four little ducks, three little ducks, two little ducks, and then continue:)

One little duck went out to play, over the hill and far away.

When mother duck went *quack, quack, quack,*

No little ducks came waddling back.

When mother duck went *quack, quack, quack,*

No little ducks came waddling back.

Then mother duck went *QUACK!, QUACK!, QUACK!*

And five little ducks came waddling back.

HEAD, SHOULDERS, KNEES, AND TOES

Head, shoulders, knees, and toes,

Knees and toes, knees and toes.

Head, shoulders, knees, and toes,

Eyes and ears and mouth and nose.

(Children tap each body part as it is mentioned. Start slowly and gradually increase the speed!)

MONTHS OF THE YEAR

Learn a poem to help remember the months of the year in order.

In January falls the snow.

In February cold winds blow.

March brings out the early flowers.

April brings the sunny showers.

In May the roses bloom so gay.

In June the farmer cuts his hay.

In July brightly shines the sun.

In August harvest has begun.

September turns the green leaves brown.

October winds then blow them down.

November days are dark and drear.

December comes and ends the year.

FIVE SPECKLED FROGS

Five little speckled frogs,

Sitting on a speckled log,

Eating the most delicious bugs,

Yum, yum, yum!

One frog jumped in the pool,

Where it was nice and cool,

Glub, glub, glub!

Now there are four speckled frogs.

Four little speckled frogs,

Sitting on a speckled log,

Eating the most delicious bugs,

Yum, yum, yum!

One frog jumped in the pool,

Where it was nice and cool,

Glub, glub, glub!

Now there are three speckled frogs.

Three little speckled frogs…

COUNTING CHANTS

1 potato, 2 potatoes,

3 potatoes, 4,

5 potatoes, 6 potatoes,

7 potatoes more.

....

1, 2, buckle my shoe,

3, 4, shut the door,

5, 6, pick up sticks,

7, 8, lay them straight,

9, 10, a big fat hen!

....

1, 2, 3, 4, 5,

I caught a fish alive,

6, 7, 8, 9, 10,

I let it go again.

Why did I let it go?

Because it bit my finger so!

Which finger did it bite?

The little one on the right!

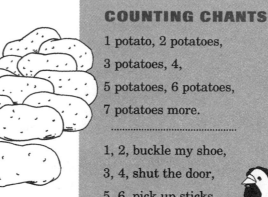

101 BOTTLES OF POP

101 bottles of pop on the wall,

101 bottles of pop.

If one of those bottles should happen to fall,

100 bottles of pop on the wall.

100 bottles of pop on the wall,

100 bottles of pop.

If one of those bottles should happen to fall,

99 bottles of pop on the wall…

(And so on!)

Additional Activities and Games for the Classroom

Bead Fun—INDEPENDENT ACTIVITY *(early in year)*

Make counting strings out of shoelaces by attaching a label with dots or a numeral on it at one end of each lace. Have children string these laces with large beads, matching the numbers of beads to the numbers of dots or to the numerals.

Puzzle Match-Ups—INDEPENDENT ACTIVITY *(early in year)*

Materials large tagboard cards or file cards; pictures of sets of objects

Paste a picture on one-half of each card and write a number from 0 to 10 on the other half that matches the number of objects in the picture. Then cut each card into two pieces, using different patterns so that each card piece will fit only its matching half. For example, a picture of three things should match only the half that has the number 3 written on it. Have children match objects with numerals.

Variation Children can make these puzzle match-ups themselves by drawing or pasting the pictures on the cards and writing the numbers, and you do the cutting.

Sticks and Cans—INDEPENDENT ACTIVITY *(early in year)*

Provide juice cans labeled with small numbers or dot sets. Have children match the labels with the correct numbers of craft sticks. Later in the year, label the cans with 2-digit numbers for children to match with bundles of ten plus additional craft sticks.

Counting-On Cards—INDEPENDENT ACTIVITY *(early in year)*

Make several sets of number cards, each set beginning with a different number and increasing by one and each set a different color. For example, use the numbers 0–10, 4–12, or 15–25, depending on the abilities of your children. Shuffle each deck. A child puts a set of cards in correct numerical order, mixes them up again, and then leaves them ready for the next player.

Number of the Day *(early in year)*

Designate a Number of the Day for each of ten days using the numbers 11 through 20.

Each day, count to form groups of various objects, using the number of the day. Eat a cracker in that many bites. Do physical actions that number of times. Divide into groups or teams of that number for various activities. Take turns writing the number on the chalkboard. Do a dot-to-dot trace from 1 to the number (put a green dot at the start).

Estimation: How Many in the Jar? *(middle of year)*

Materials a jar containing small objects, such as centimeter cubes, pennies, marbles, or edible snacks

Children guess the number of objects in the jar and write their guesses on paper. If a number line is used, children tape their answers to it. Children read their own guesses. Take out the objects while children help you count them. If the objects are edible, they can be divided among the children and eaten.

If you have a large number of objects in the jar, it may help children to see a jar of the same size containing fewer objects and labeled with the correct number for reference.

Repeat this activity periodically using objects of different sizes. As a variation, use two jars of equal size and put larger objects in one and smaller objects in the other. Have children guess which jar holds more objects and then count to verify.

Fist Stacking *(middle of year)*

Ask: *How many children do we need to have seven fists?* Then have children act out the situation as a fist-stacking game by taking turns placing one fist on top of the other: first fist, and then a second fist, and so on until there are seven fists.

Estimating Letter Use Frequency *(middle of year)*

Put children's names on a name chart large enough for all to see. Then ask children to estimate which letter of the alphabet appears most often in all their names. Record estimates and then count or tally the results.

Time Chart Game *(late in year)*

Materials two 1-inch cubes marked with digital times to the hour, one marked with times 1:00–6:00 and the other with times 7:00–12:00; copies of Activity Masters 37 and 38 (Clock Faces 1:00–6:00 and 7:00–12:00); game markers (such as washers, pebbles, or chips). Cut and paste the clock faces to cardboard or posterboard to make different game boards (with six clocks per board). Alternatively, use a clock face stamp or Activity Master 39 (Clock Faces (blank)) and draw in the hour hands for different boards.

This game can be played by 2 to 4 players.

Each player has a game board with six clocks showing different (hour) times. Players take turns rolling one of the two marked cubes. After each roll, all players look for clocks on their game boards that show the time rolled, and each player who finds one covers that clock with a marker.

The winner can be the first person to cover all the clocks on his or her game board, or play continues until all players have covered all their clocks.

Sticky Line Game *(late in year)*

Materials two sets of number cards, one marked with the numbers +1 through +10 and the other marked with the numbers −1 through −10

This activity may work best with a small group (15 children or so).

Line children up along the edge of the rug or any "line" in the classroom that's away from a wall. They should stand shoulder to shoulder facing you. Dramatically pretend to "glue" them to this line.

Use the two sets of number cards described above. Show one card at a time to children, either individually or as a group. A child or a group of children moves the same number of steps off the "sticky" line as the number shown on the card, forward for positive (+) numbers or backward for negative (−) numbers. Children are "stuck" until they respond correctly to the cards that you show them. If they take the wrong number of steps, they must return to the line and be stuck again.

Continue until each child has had a few turns with different types of cards.

Egg-Carton Mathematics—ADDITION AND SUBTRACTION

NUMBER MODELS *(late in year)*

Write a simple number model (such as 3 + 2 or 5 − 4) on the top of each cup of an egg carton. Children work out the problems with beans and then show the answers by putting numbered pieces of cardboard in the correct cups.

Children's Books That Include Mathematics

Numeration

Anno, Mitsumasa. *Anno's Counting Book*. New York: HarperCollins, 1987.

Bang. *Ten, Nine, Eight*. New York: William Morrow & Co., 1998.

Bishop, Claire Huchet and Kurt Weise. *The Five Chinese Brothers*. New York: Putnam, 1988.

Carle, Eric. *1, 2, 3 to the Zoo: A Counting Book*. New York: Philomel Books, 1996.

——. *Rooster's Off to See the World*. New York: Simon & Schuster, 1987.

——. *The Very Hungry Caterpillar*. New York: Philomel Books, 1994.

Cave, Kathryn. *Out for the Count: A Counting Adventure*. Vermont: Frances Lincoln, 2000.

Crews, Donald. *Ten Black Dots*. New York: William Morrow & Co., 1995.

Ehlert, Lois. *Fish Eyes: A Book You Can Count On*. San Diego: Harcourt Brace, 1992.

Feelings, Muriel. *Mojo Means One: A Swahili Counting Book*. New York: Dial Press, 1989.

Geisel, Theodore Seuss. *One Fish Two Fish Red Fish Blue Fish*. New York: Random House, 1981.

Grossman, Virginia. *Ten Little Rabbits*. San Francisco: Chronicle Books, 1995.

Hayes, Sarah. *Nine Ducks Nine*. Cambridge, MA: Candlewick Press, 1996.

Hoban, Tana. *Count and See*. New York: Simon & Schuster, 1972.

Kasza, Keiko. *The Wolf's Chicken Stew*. New York: Putnam, 1987.

Keats, Ezra Jack. *Over in the Meadow*. New York: Puffin, 1999.

Mahy, Margaret. *17 Kings and 42 Elephants*. New York: Dial Books, 1993.

Mathews, Louise. *Bunches and Bunches of Bunnies*. New York: Scholastic, 1989.

Merriam, Eve. *12 Ways to Get to 11*. New York: Simon & Schuster, 1996.

Munsch, Robert. *Moira's Birthday*. Toronto: Annick Press, 1989.

Oughton, Jerrie. *How the Stars Fell into the Sky: A Navajo Legend*. Boston: Houghton Mifflin, 1992

Robbins, Ruth. *Baboushka and the Three Kings*. Boston: Houghton Mifflin, 1960.

Ryan, Pam Munoz. *The Crayon Counting Book*. Watertown, MA: Charlesbridge Publishing, 1996.

Sendak, Maurice. *One Was Johnny*. New York: HarperCollins, 1962.

——. *Seven Little Monsters*. New York: HarperCollins, 1977.

Sheppard, Jeff. *The Right Number of Elephants*. New York: HarperCollins, 1992.

Slobodkina, Esphyr. *Caps for Sale*. New York: HarperCollins, 1985.

Tildes, Phyllis Limbacher. *Counting on Calico*. Watertown, MA: Charlesbridge Publishing, 1995.

Tudor, Tasha. *1 is One*. New York: Simon & Schuster, 2000.

Walsh, Ellen Stoll. *Mouse Count*. New York: Voyager Books, 1995.

Measurement

Eastman, Phillip D. *Big Dog…Little Dog: A Bedtime Story*. New York: Random House, 1973.

Hoban, Tana. *Is It Larger? Is It Smaller?*. New York: William Morrow & Co., 1997.

Kellogg, Steven. *Much Bigger Than Martin*. New York: Dial Books for Young Readers, 1992.

Lionni, Leo. *Inch by Inch*. New York: William Morrow & Co., 1995.

Murphy, Stuart J. *The Best Bug Parade*. New York: Harper Trophy, 1996.

Myller, Rolf. *How Big Is a Foot?* New York: Dell Publishing, 1991.

Geometry

Carle, Eric. *The Secret Birthday Message*. New York: HarperCollins, 1972.

Dodds, Dayle Ann. *The Shape of Things*. Cambridge, MA: Candlewick Press, 1996.

Friedman, Aileen. *A Cloak for a Dreamer*. New York: Scholastic, 1995.

Grifalconi, Ann. *The Village of Round and Square Houses*. Boston: Little Brown, 1986.

Hoban, Tana. *Big Ones, Little Ones*. New York: William Morrow & Co., 1976.

——. *So Many Circles, So Many Squares*. New York: Greenwillow Books, 1998.

——. *Cubes, Cones, Cylinders, and Spheres*. New York: Greenwillow Books, 2000.

——. *Shapes, Shapes, Shapes*. New York: William Morrow & Co., 1986.

MacDonald, Suse. *Sea Shapes*. San Diego: Gulliver Books, 1994.

Tompert, Ann. *Grandfather Tang's Story*. New York: Crown Publishers, 1990.

Operations

Adler, David A. *Fraction Fun*. New York: Holiday House. 1997.

Giganti, Paul. *Each Orange Had 8 Slices: A Counting Book*. New York: Greenwillow Books, 1992.

Hutchins, Pat. *The Doorbell Rang*. New York: William Morrow & Co., 1989.

Leedy, Loreen. *Fraction Action*. New York: Holiday House. 1994.

McMillan, Bruce. *Eating Fractions*. New York: Scholastic, 1991.

Murphy, Stuart J. *Elevator Magic*. New York: HarperCollins, 1997.

Pinczes, Elinor J. *One Hundred Hungry Ants*. Boston: Houghton Mifflin Company, 1993.

——. *A Remainder of One*. Boston, Houghton Mifflin Company, 1995.

Patterns and Functions

Cleveland, David. *April Rabbits*. New York: Scholastic, Inc., 1989.

Chicken Licken

McClintock, Mike. *A Fly Went By*. New York: Random House, 1987.

The Gingerbread Boy

Silverstein, Shel. *Giraffe and a Half*. New York: HarperCollins, 1981.

The House That Jack Built

Lazy Jack

The Little Red Hen

The Old Woman and Her Pig

Money

Brisson, Pat. *Benny's Pennies*. New York: Dell Publishing, 1995.

Schwartz, David M. *If You Made a Million*. New York: Lothrop, Lee & Shepard, 1989.

Viorst, Judith. *Alexander, Who Used to Be Rich Last Sunday*. New York: Atheneum, 1978.

Williams, Vera. *A Chair for My Mother*. New York: Greenwillow Books, 1983.

Clocks and Calendars

Anno, Mitsumasa. *All in a Day*. New York: Putnam, 1999.

Hutchins, Pat. *Clocks and More Clocks*. New York: Simon & Schuster, 1994.

Llewellyn, Claire. *My First Book of Time*. New York: Dorling-Kindersley, 1992.

Sendak, Maurice. *Chicken Soup with Rice*. New York: HarperCollins, 1962.

Williams, Vera B. *Three Days on a River in a Red Canoe*. New York: Greenwillow Books, 1984.

Zolotow, Charlotte. *Over and Over*. New York: Harper Trophy, 1995.

Data and Chance

Murphy, Stuart J. *Lemonade for Sale*. New York: HarperCollins, 1998.

——. *The Best Vacation Ever*. New York: Harper Trophy, 1997.

Big Numbers

Anno, Masaichiro. *Anno's Mysterious Multiplying Jar*. New York: Putnam, 1999.

Gag Wanda. *Millions of Cats*. New York: Putnam, 1996.

McKissack, Patricia. *A Million Fish...More or Less*. Random House, 1996.

Schwartz, David M. *How Much Is a Million?* New York: William Morrow & Co., 1994.

Numbers in Fairy Tales

Cinderella

Little One Eye, Little Two Eye, Little Three Eye

Little Red Riding Hood

Snow White and the Seven Dwarfs

The Three Bears

The Three Billy Goats Gruff

The Three Little Pigs

Thumbelina

The Tiny Tiny Woman

The Twelve Dancing Princesses

The Wolf and the Seven Little Kids

Wordless Books

(These books have such vivid details in the illustrations that they are excellent for observing and counting.)

Anno, Mitsumasa, *Anno's Journey*. New York: Putnam, 1997.

Briggs, Raymond. *Father Christmas*. New York: Random House, 1997.

de Paola, Tomie. *Pancakes for Breakfast*. New York: Harcourt Brace, 1990.

——. *The Hunter and the Animals*. New York: Holiday House, 1981.

Hutchins, Pat. *Changes, Changes*. New York: Simon & Schuster, 1987.

Kosowsky, Cindy. *Wordless Counting Book*. Bridgeport, CT: Greene Bark Press, 1993.

Spier, Peter. *Noah's Ark*. New York: Dell Publishing, 1992.

Commercial Games That Use Mathematics

COUNTING

Candy Land

Chutes and Ladders

Cubits

Hi-Ho! Cherry-O

Shut the Box

Sorry

Three Readiness Math Games

ATTRIBUTES, PATTERNS, GEOMETRY

Guess Who

mazes

Peanut Butter and Jelly

Polydrones

puzzles

Tangoes

tangrams

STRATEGY

The Amazing Labyrinth

Battleship

checkers

chess

Chinese checkers

Connect Four

Hen Berta

Junior Monopoly

Mancala

Memory

Milles Bournes

Othello

Princess

Activities by Strand

Note: Activity titles printed in boldface type indicate Core Activities. See page 18 for more information.

Glossary for Teachers

addend   One of two or more numbers that are added. For example, in 5 + 3 + 1, the addends are 5,3, and 1.

addition   A mathematical operation based on putting together two or more quantities. Numbers being added are called *addends*; the result of addition is called the *sum*. For example, in 12 + 33 = 45, 12 and 33 are addends and 45 is the sum. Subtraction "undoes" addition: 12 + 33 = 45 can be "undone" by 45 − 12 = 33 or 45 − 33 = 12.

analog clock   A clock that shows the time by the positions of the hour and minute hands (and sometimes a hand for seconds). Compare to *digital clock*.

analog clock

array   A rectangular arrangement of objects in rows and columns.

array

attribute   A feature of an object or common feature of a set of objects. Example of attributes include size, shape, color, and number of sides.

bank draft   A written order for the exchange of money. $1,000 bills are no longer circulated so *Kindergarten Everyday Mathematics* uses $1,000 bank drafts.

bar graph   A graph that shows the relationships among data by the use of bars to represent quantities.

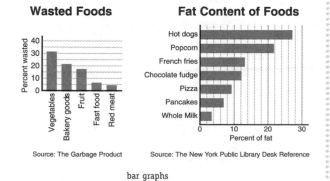

bar graphs

calendar   (1) A reference frame used to keep track of the passage of time. Many different calendars exist, including the Gregorian calendar that most of the Western world currently uses, the Hebrew calendar, the Islamic calendar, and others.
(2) The concrete representation of such a reference frame, on which appointments, special days, and other markings can be made.
(3) A schedule or listing of events.

cent   1) One-hundredth, (with a penny; $\frac{1}{100}$ of a dollar). The word comes from the Latin word *centesimus*, which means *hundredth part*.

(2) A prefix meaning one hundred, as in *century*

centimeter (cm)   In the metric system, a unit of length equivalent to 10 millimeters, $\frac{1}{10}$ of a decimeter, and $\frac{1}{100}$ of a meter.

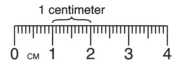

chance   The possibility of an outcome occuring in an uncertain event; for example, in tossing a coin there is an equal chance of getting heads or tails.

circle   The set of all points in a plane that are equally distant from a given point in the plane called the *center* of the circle. The distance from the center to the circle is the *radius*. The circle is the boundary only. A circle together with its interior is called a *disk* or a circular *region*.

circle

column   A vertical arrangement of objects or numbers in an array or table.

cone   A 3-dimensional shape having a circular base, a curved surface, and one vertex, called the *apex*.

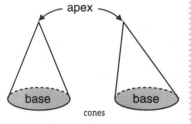

cones

counting numbers   The numbers used to count things. The set of counting numbers is {1,2,3,4, ...}. Sometimes 0 is included.

cube   A regular polyhedron with six square faces.

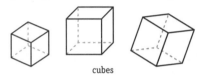

cubes

cup   In the U.S. customary system, a unit of capacity equal to 8 fluid ounces; $\frac{1}{2}$ pint.

cylinder   A 3-dimensional shape having a curved surface and parallel circular or elliptical bases that are the same size. A can is a common object shaped like a cylinder.

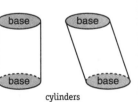

cylinders

data   Information gathered by observing, counting, or measuring. Strictly, *data* is the plural of *datum*, but *data* is often used as a singular word.

decade   A group or set of 10, as in a period of ten years.

degree Celsius (°C)   Unit for marking Celsius thermometers or for measuring differences in temperature in the metric system. On the Celsius scale, pure water at sea level freezes at 0° and boils at 100°.

degree Fahrenheit (°F)   Unit for marking Fahrenheit thermometers or measuring differences in temperature in the U.S. customary system. On the Fahrenheit scale, pure water at sea level freezes at 32° and boils at 212°F, while a saturated salt solution freezes at 0°F.

difference   The amount by which one number is greater than or less than another number; the result of counting between the two numbers or subtracting one

number from another. For example, in $12 - 5 = 7$, 7 is the difference between 5 and 12.

digit   In the base-10 numeration system, one of the symbols 0, 1, 2, 3, 4, 5, 6, 7, 8, 9, which can be used to write any number. For example, the numeral 145 is made up of the digits 1, 4, and 5.

digital clock   A clock that shows the time with numbers to represent hours and minutes (and sometimes seconds), with a colon separating the two. Compare to *analog clock*.

digital clock

dollar   Basic unit of money in the U.S. money system, equal to 100 cents.

equivalent   Equal in value, but possibly different in form. For example, $\frac{1}{2}$, 0.5, and 50% are equivalent.

equivalent names   Different ways of naming the same number. For example: $2 + 6$, $4 + 4$, $12 - 4$, $18 - 0$, $100 - 92$, $5 + 1 + 2$, eight, VIII, and ⊬⊬ /// are all equivalent names for 8.

estimate   (1) (noun) A close, rather than exact, answer; an approximate answer to a computation; a number close to another number. (2) (verb) To make an estimate.

foot (ft)   In the U.S. customary system, a unit of length equivalent to 12 inches or $\frac{1}{3}$ of a yard.

fraction   A number in the form $\frac{a}{b}$ or a/b, where a and b are whole numbers and b is not 0. Fractions are used in many contexts—to name part of an object or part of a collection of objects, to compare two quantities, and to represent division.

fulcrum   (1) The center support of a rocker or pan balance. (2) The support on which a lever turns.

fulcrum

fulcrum

function A set of pairs of input and output numbers created by a specific rule. The same input cannot lead to more than one output. The pairs can be shown in a table (see below), as points on a coordinate graph, or by the rule that creates them. For example, for a function with a rule of "double," 1 is paired with 2, 2 is paired with 4, 3 is paired with 6, and so on.

function machine In *Everyday Mathematics,* a diagram of an imaginary machine programmed to process numbers according to a certain rule. A number (input) is put into the machine and is then transformed into a second number (output) through the application of a rule.

in	out
1	2
2	4
3	6
5	10
20	40
300	600

function machine

geometric solid A 3-dimensional shape bounded by surfaces. Common geometric solids include *rectangular prisms, square-based pyramids, cylinders, cones, and spheres.*

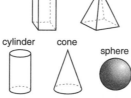

geometric solids

geometry The study of spatial objects, their properties, and relationships; the word geometry is derived from the Greek words for "earth" and "measure."

half One of two equal parts.

height A measure of how tall something is.

hexagon A 6-sided polygon.

Home Link In *Everyday Mathematics,* a suggested follow-up or enrichment activity to be done at home.

hexagon

horizontal Positioned in a left-to-right orientation; parallel to the line of the horizon.

inch (in.) In the U.S. customary system, a unit of length equal to $\frac{1}{12}$ of a foot and defined as equal to 2.54 centimeters.

kite A quadrilateral with exactly two pairs of adjacent sides that are the same length. (A rhombus is not a kite.) Compare to *rhombus.*

kite

label A descriptive word or phrase used to put a number or numbers in context. Using a label reinforces the idea that numbers refer to something. Flags, snowballs, and scary monsters are examples of labels.

line of symmetry A line that divides a figure into two halves that are mirror images of each other. Each point in one of the halves of the figure is the same distance from the line of symmetry as the corresponding point in the other half. A figure may have any number of lines of symmetry. For example, a parallelogram that is not a rectangle or a rhombus has no lines of symmetry. A square has four lines of symmetry.

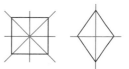

lines of symmetry

mathematics A study of relationships among numbers, shapes, systems, and patterns. Mathematics is used to count and measure things, to discover similarities and differences, to solve problems, and to learn about and organize the world.

measurement unit The reference unit used when measuring. Basic units include meters (length), kilograms (mass or weight), liters (capacity), seconds (elapsed time), and degrees Celsius (change of temperature). Compound units include such things as square centimeters (area) and kilometers per hour (speed).

meter (m) In the metric system, the fundamental unit of length from which other metric units of length are derived. One meter is equal to 10 decimeters, 100 centimeters, and 1000 millimeters.

name collection A collection of equivalent names for a number. A name collection for 5 might include 4 + 1, 3 + 2, and so on.

negative number A number less than 0; a number to the left of 0 on a horizontal number line or below 0 on a thermometer or other vertical number line.

number grid In *Everyday Mathematics,* a table in which consecutive numbers are arranged in rows; usually of ten. A move from one number to the next within a row is a change of 1; a move from one number to the next within a column is a change of 10.

number grid

number line   A line on which points correspond to numbers, used as a frame of reference for counting and numeration activities. Every number has a point on the line, and every point has a number.

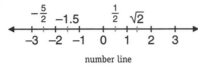

number line

number model   A number sentence that models or fits a situation. For example, the situation "Sally had $5. Then she earned $8," "A young plant 5 cm high grew 8 cm," and "Harry is 8 years older than his 5-year-old sister, Sally" can all be modeled by the number sentence $5 + 8 = 13$.

number story   A story that contains a problem that can be solved using one or more of the four basic arithmetic operations or by sorting out relations such as equals, is less than, or is greater than.

numeration   The study of numbers—their meaning, representation, and relationships. In *Everyday Mathematics,* numeration activities include counting, writing numbers, comparing numbers, identifying equivalent forms of numbers, and exchanging coins (such as, 5 pennies for 1 nickel).

octagon   An 8-sided polygon.

octagons

operation   An action performed on one or two numbers producing a single number result.

ordinal number   A number used to express position or order in a series, such as first, third, or tenth. Generally, ordinal numbers are used to name dates— for example, people say "May fifth," (rather than "May five")

parallelogram   A quadrilateral that has two pairs of parallel sides and opposite sides that are congruent. All rectangles are parallelograms, but not all parallelograms are rectangles, since some parallelograms do not have right angles.

pattern   A model or plan by which objects or numbers can be arranged so that what comes next can be predicted.

Pattern-Block Template   In *Everyday Mathematics,* a sheet of plastic with geometric shapes cut out, used to draw patterns and designs.

pentagon   A 5-sided polygon.

pentagons

perimeter   The distance around a closed plane figure or region. *Peri-* comes from the Greek word for "around" and *-meter* comes from the Greek word for "measure"; perimeter means "around measure."

pictograph   A graph constructed with pictures or symbols. A pictograph makes it possible to compare at a glance the relative amounts of two or more counts or measures.

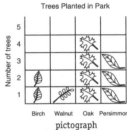

pictograph

place value   The relative worth of each digit in a number, which is determined by its position. Each place has a value ten times that of the place to its right and one-tenth of the value of the place to its left.

polygon   A closed plane figure formed by three or more line segments that meet only at their endpoints. The word comes from Greek: *poly* means many, and *-gon* (from *gonia,* means angle).

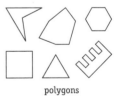

polygons

polyhedron   A closed 3-dimensional shape, all of whose surfaces (faces) are flat. Each face consists of a polygon and the interior of the polygon.

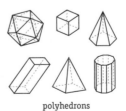

polyhedrons

positive number
A number greater than 0; a number to the right of 0 on a horizontal number line or above 0 on a thermometer or other vertical number line.

quadrangle A 4-sided polygon. Same as *quadrilateral*.

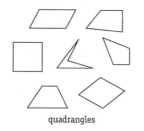
quadrangles

quadrilateral A 4-sided polygon. Same as *quadrangle*.

rational counting Counting using one-to-one matching, such as counting a number of objects (the number of chairs, people, crackers, and so on.)

rectangle A parallelogram whose angles are all right angles. See *parallelogram*.

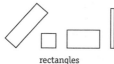
rectangles

reference frame A system for locating numbers within a given context, often with reference to an arbitrarily set 0-point. Examples of reference frames are number lines, timelines, calendar systems and temperature scales.

rhombus A parallelogram with sides that are all the same length. The angles may be right angles, in which case the rhombus is a square.

rhombuses

scale (1) A number line on a thermometer used for measuring temperature.
(2) An instrument for measuring weight.

second (1) A unit of time. There are 60 seconds in a minute.
(2) An ordinal number in the sequence first, second, third, ….

skip count Counting by certain regular intervals, such as 2s, 5s, or 10s. For example, 2, 4, 6, 8, 10, 12, and so on.

slate A lap-sized (about 8" by 11") chalkboard or whiteboard that children use in *Everyday Mathematics* for a variety of purposes, including recording responses during group exercises and informal group assessments.

speed A rate that compares distance traveled with the time taken to travel that distance.

square A rectangle whose sides are all the same length.

squares

standard unit A unit of measure that has been defined by a recognized authority, such as a government or standards organization. For example, centimeters, inches, miles, and seconds are all standard units.

subitizing To perceive at a glance the number of items presented. For example, a child can tell you immediately that you are holding up three fingers but will probably need to count them if you hold up eight.

subtraction The operation used to find how many are left when some are taken away, when a given quantity is decreased, or when comparing quantities. The number being subtracted is the *subtrahend;* the number it is subtracted from is called the *minuend;* the result of subtraction is called the *difference*. For example, in $45 - 12 = 33$, 45 is the minuend, 12 is the subtrahend, and 33 is the difference. Addition "undoes" subtraction: $45 - 12 = 33$ can be "undone" by $12 + 33 = 45$.

survey A study that collects data. For example, surveys are used to find out about people's characteristics, behaviors, interests, opinions, and so on. In *Everyday Mathematics,* surveys are used to generate data for graphing and analysis.

symmetry The property of exact balance in a figure; having the same size and shape across a dividing line or around a point.

line symmetry   rotational symmetry

tally Marks used to keep track of a count, ⦀⦀⦀ ||||.

temperature A measure of how hot or cold something is, usually expressed in degrees Celsius or degrees Fahrenheit. The Celsius and Fahrenheit temperature scales are different reference frames for locating temperatures.

3-dimensional (3-D) (1) A figure in space that cannot be contained in a plane. Examples include prisms, pyramids, or spheres, all of which, roughly speaking, have length, width, and height. Other examples include intersecting planes or sets of lines that are not all in the same plane.
(2) A figure or surface on which any point can be located with three numbers in a coordinate system.

timeline A device for showing in sequence when events took place. A timeline is a number line with the numbers naming years, days, and so on.

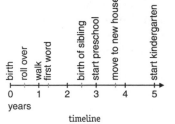

timeline

trapezoid A quadrilateral that has one pair of parallel sides. No two sides need to be the same length.

trapezoid

triangle A 3-sided polygon.

| equilateral triangle | iscoceles triangle | scalene triangle |

2-dimensional (2-D) (1) Any figure contained completely within a plane. Objects with lengths and width but no thickness.
(2) A figure or surface on which one can locate any point with two numbers in a coordinate system.

Venn diagram A picture that uses closed figures to show relationships among sets.

Girls on Sports Teams

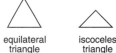

Venn diagram

vertical Upright; perpendicular to the horizon.

volume A measure of the amount of space occupied by a 3-dimensional shape, generally expressed in cubic units, such as cm³, cubic inches, or cubic feet.

weight A measure of how heavy something is. Technically, a measure of the force of gravity on an object, which is the product of its mass and the acceleration due to gravity. Hence, the same object can have different weights depending on gravity. For example, a person who weighs 150 pounds in San Diego would have a different weight on the moon and experience "weightlessness" in a spaceship.

"What's My Rule?"
In *Everyday Mathematics,* a routine that involves a set of number pairs in which the numbers in each pair are related to each other according to the same rule. "What's My Rule?" problems are usually displayed in table form in which two of the three parts (input, output, and rule) are known, and the goal is to find the unknown part.

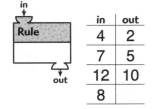

"What's My Rule?"

yard (yd) Historically, the distance from the tip of the nose to the tip of the longest finger. In the U.S. customary system, a unit of length equivalent to 3 feet or 36 inches.

Index

Activity Masters

Activity Masters (cont.)

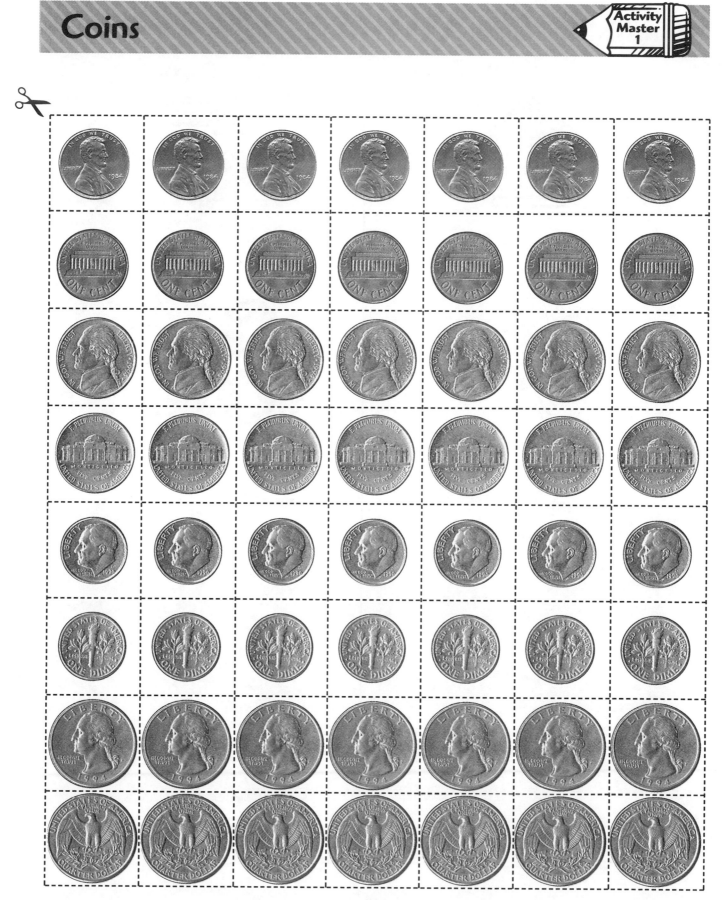

Use with activity on page 40.

Things That Float or Sink

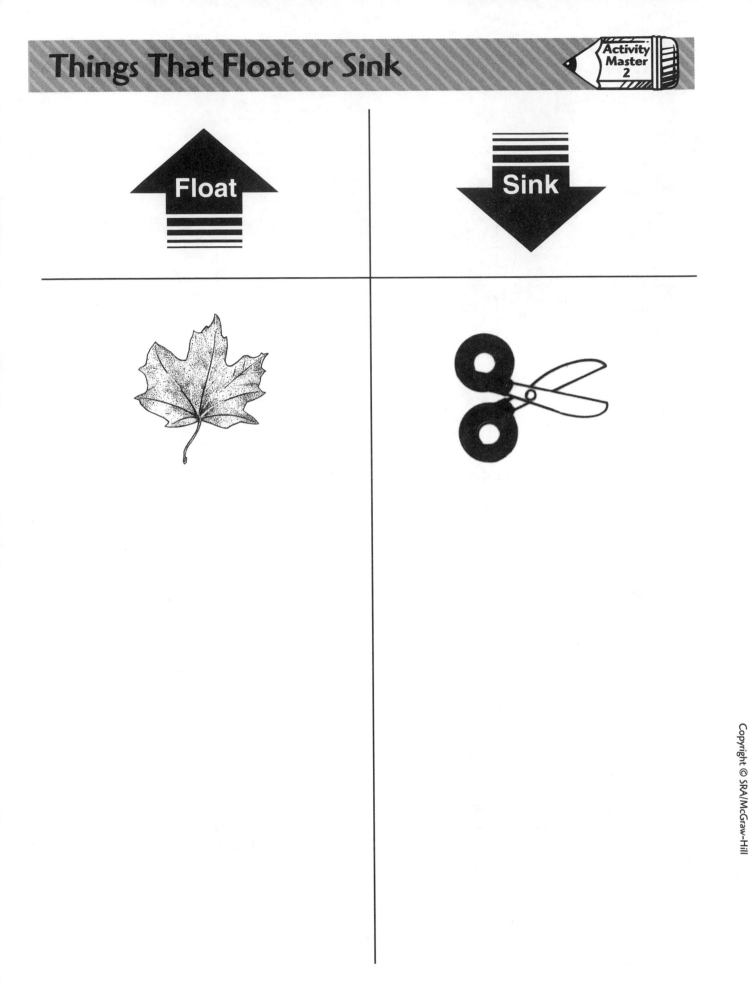

Float

Sink

Use with activity on page 47.

Activity Master 3

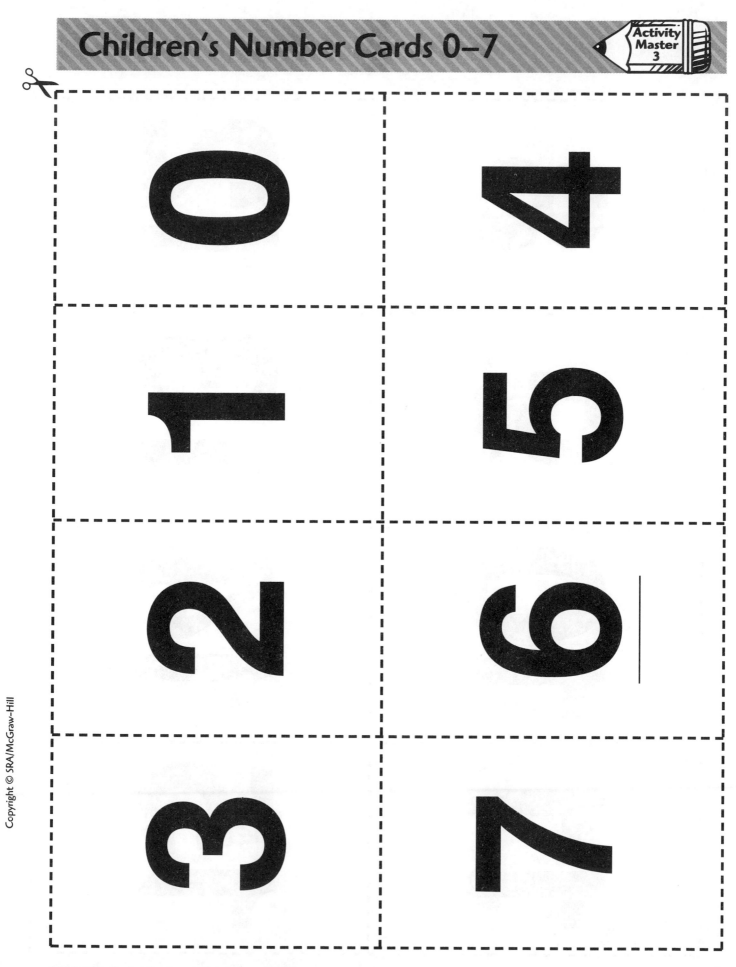

Use with activities on pages 50 and 278.

63

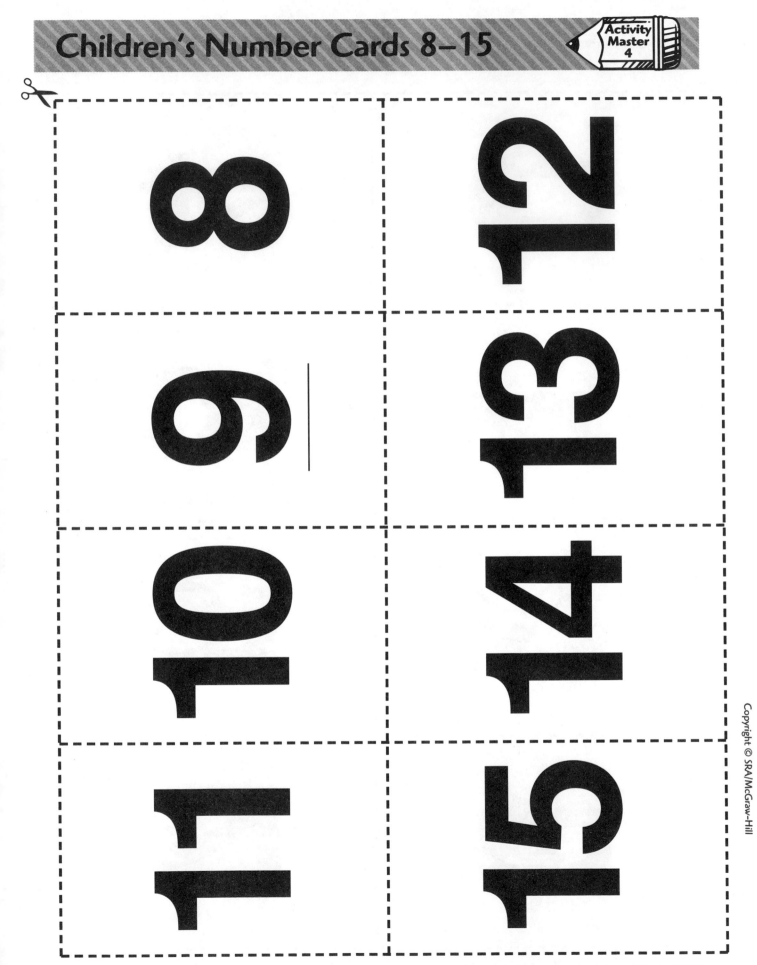

Use with activities on pages 50 and 278.

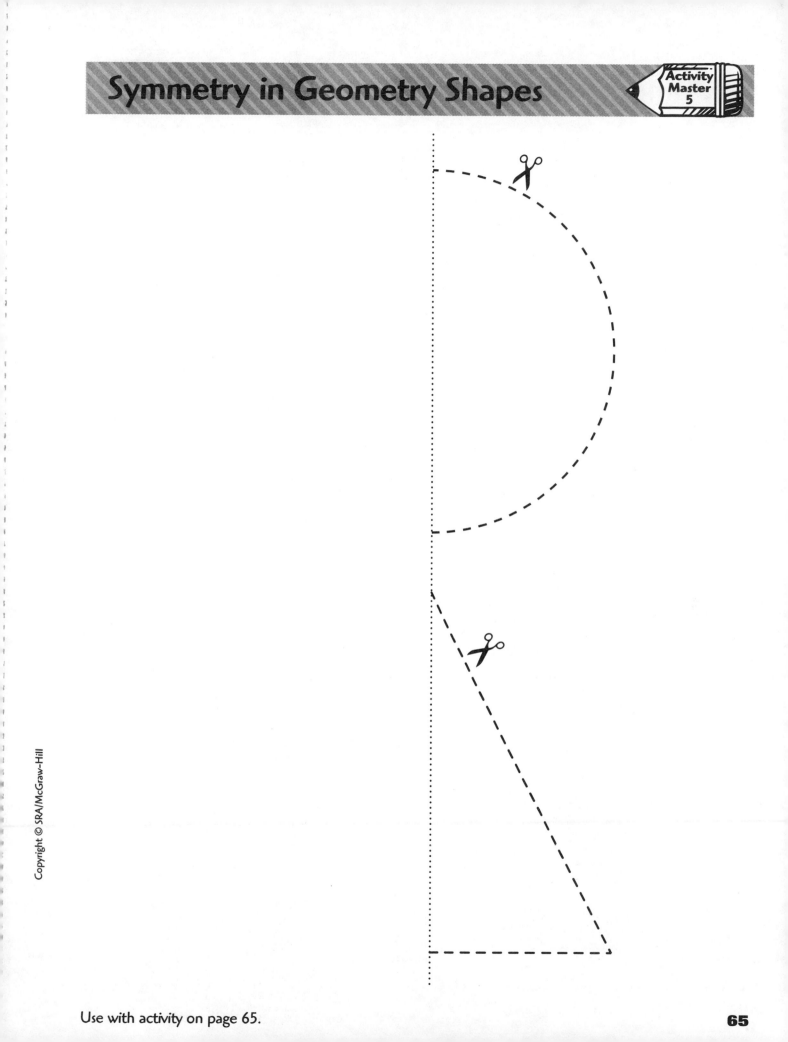

Use with activity on page 65.

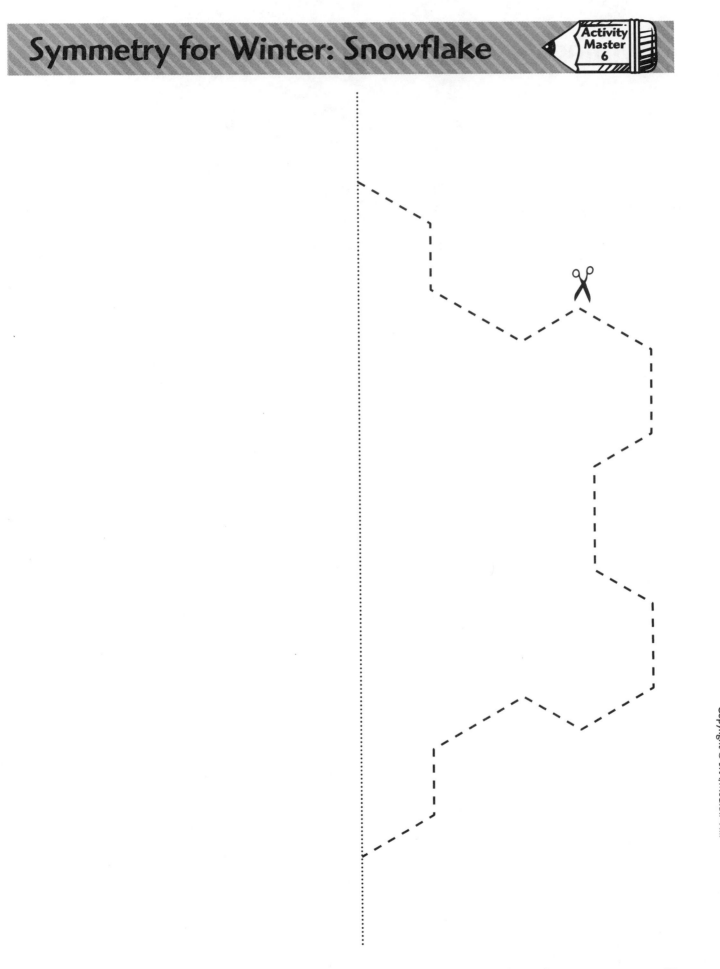

Activity
Master
6

Use with activity on page 65.

Symmetry for Valentine's Day: Heart

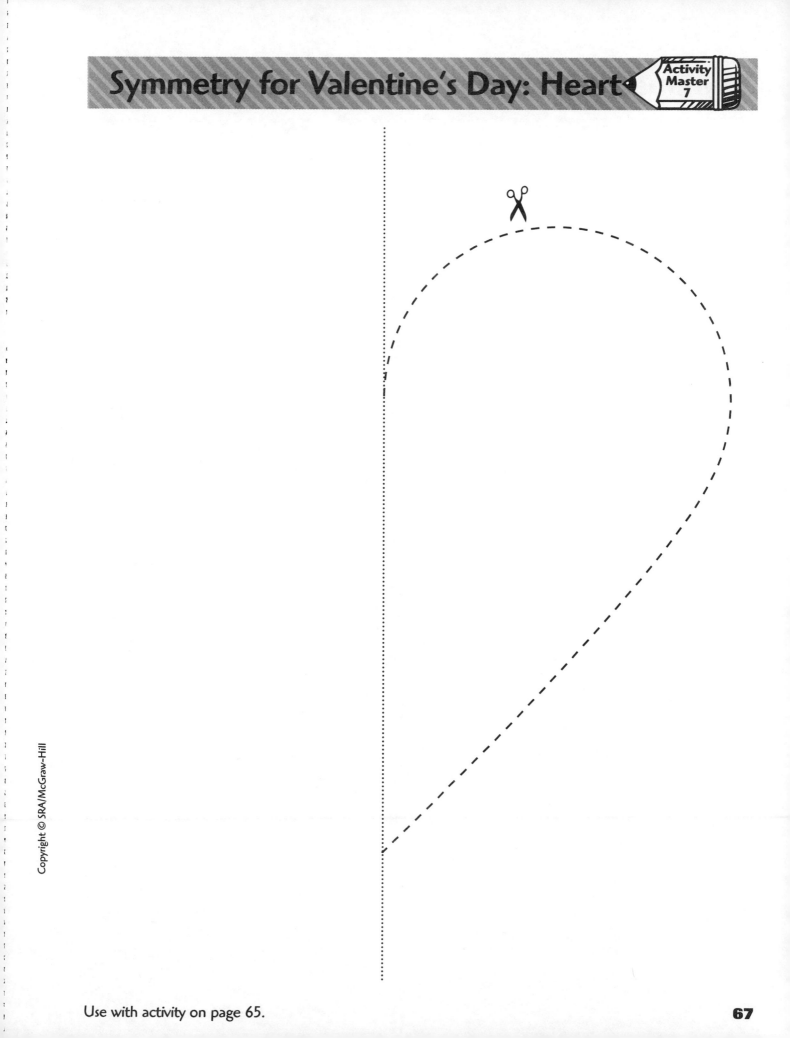

Use with activity on page 65.

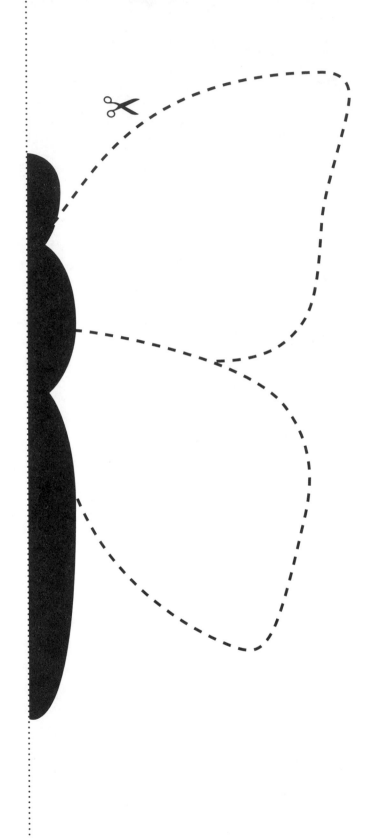

Use with activity on page 65.

Name: _____

Telephone Number: 1 – _____ – _____ – _____
(area code)

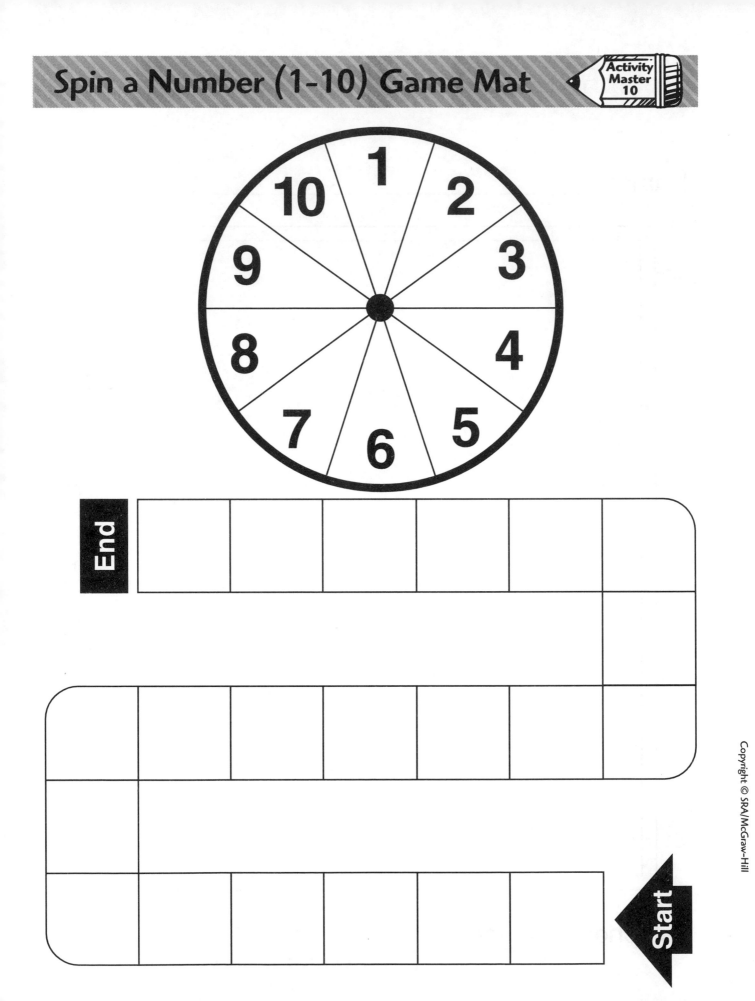

End

Start

Use with activity on page 80.

Activity Master 11

Use with activity on page 84.

71

Activity
Master
12

Use with activity on page 84.

Mini Monsters

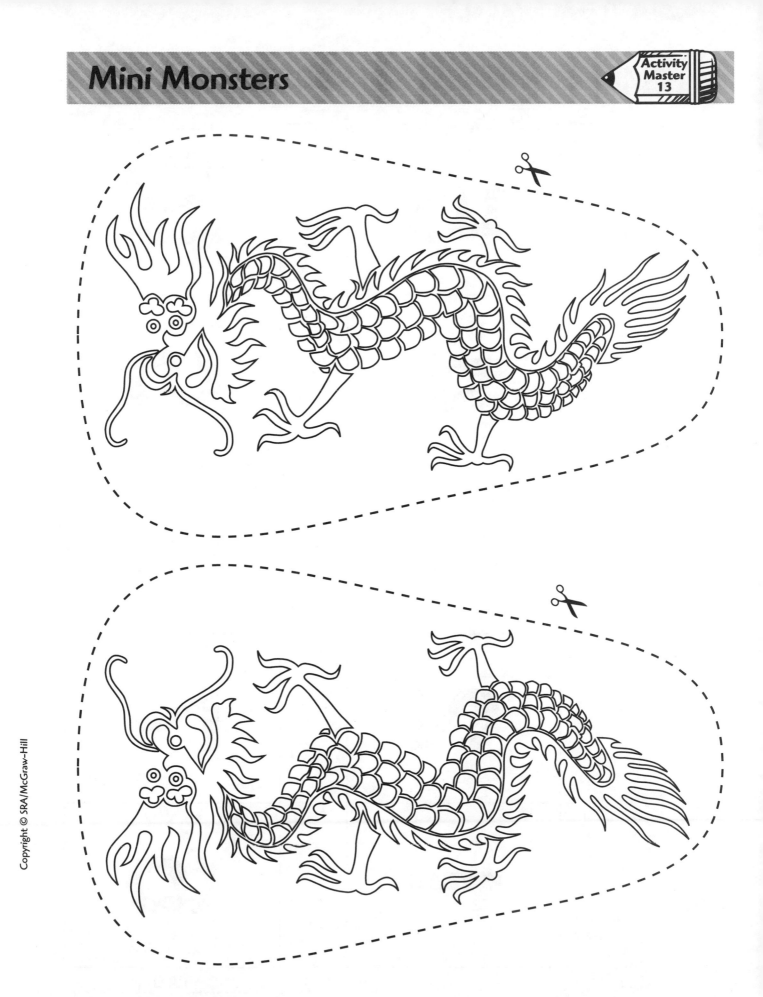

Use with activity on page 86.

73

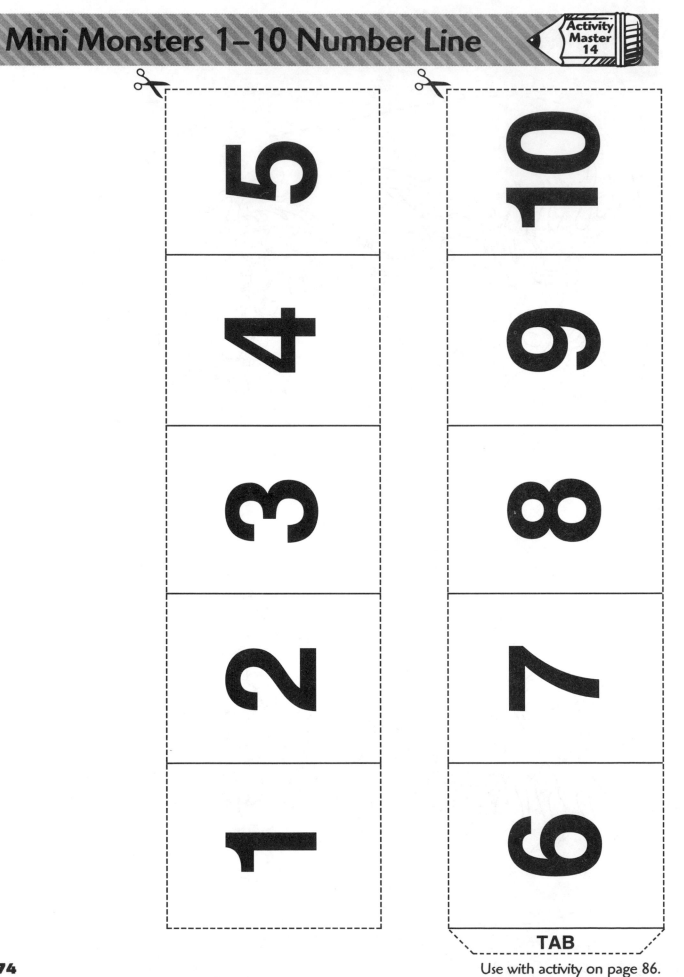

Activity Master 14

5 **4** **3** **2** **1**

10 **9** **8** **7** **6**

TAB

Use with activity on page 86.

Activity
Master
15

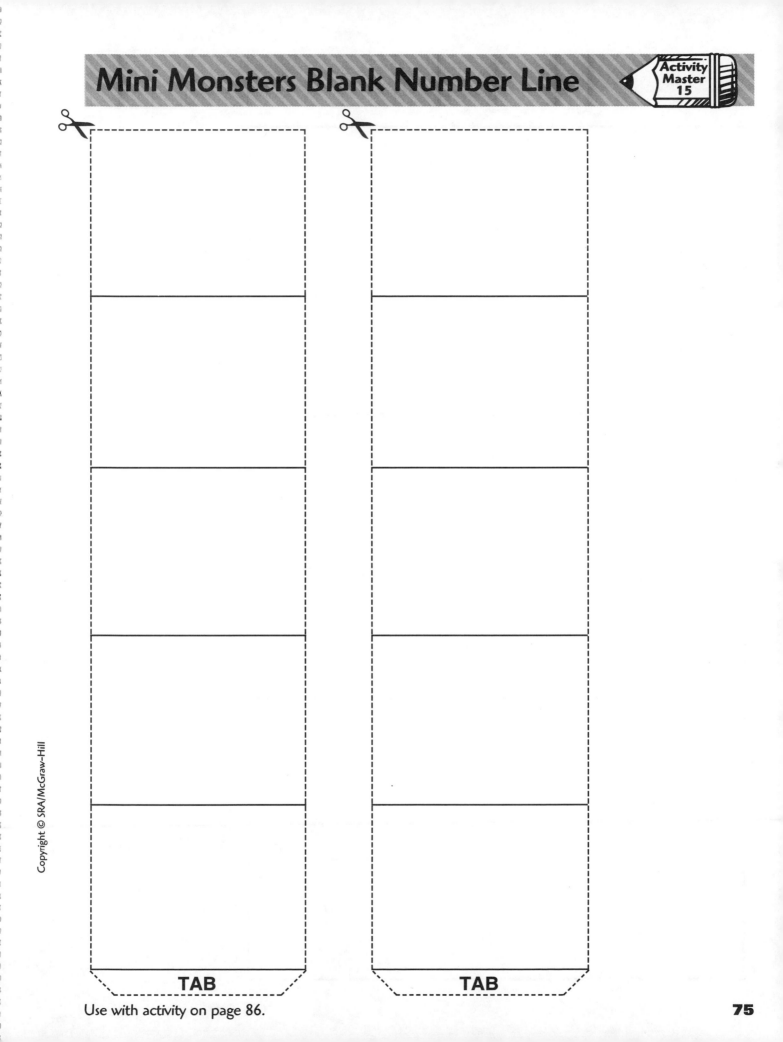

TAB

TAB

Use with activity on page 86.

Activity
Master
16

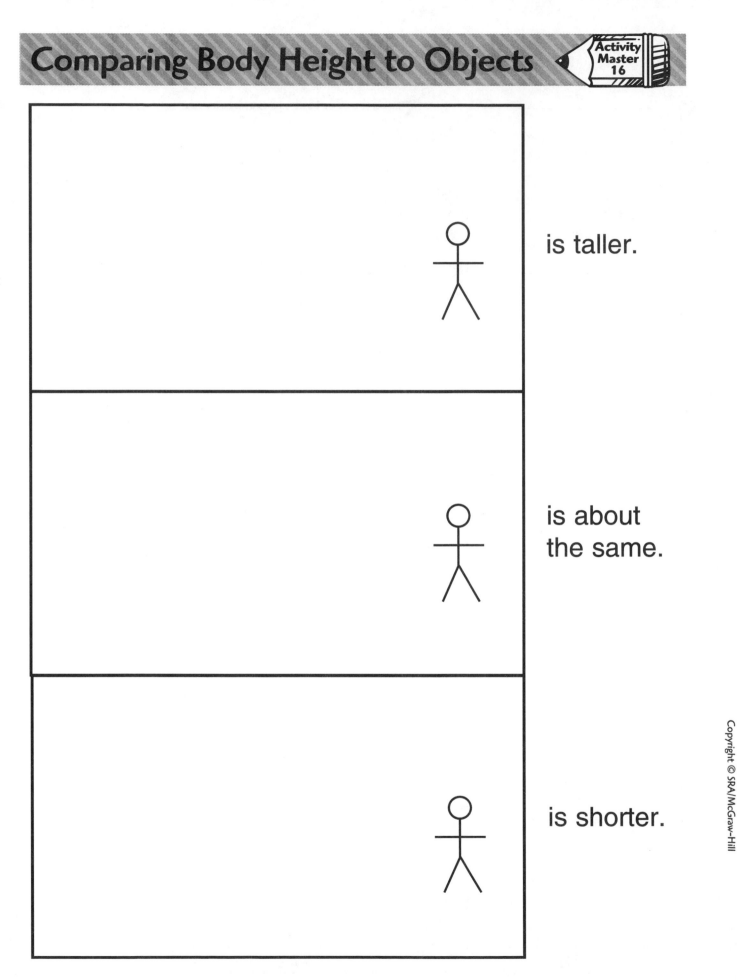

is taller.

is about
the same.

is shorter.

Use with activity on page 95.

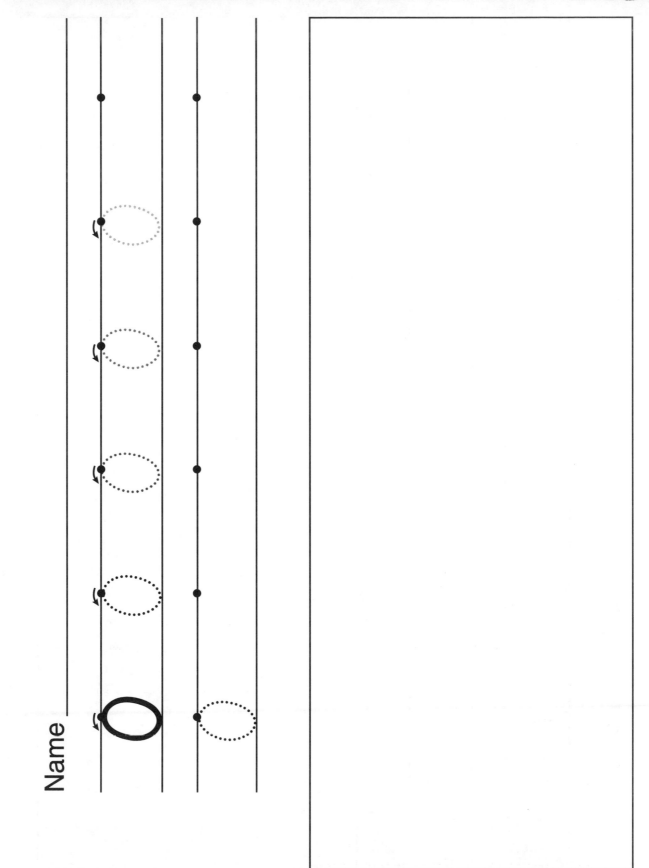

Name

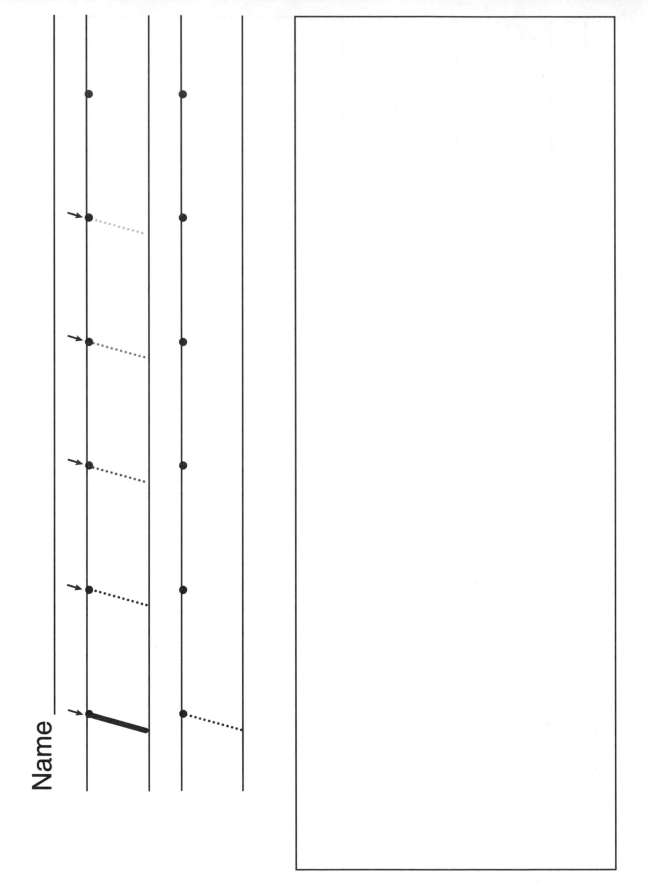

Name

Use with activity on page 112.

Number Book (2)

Name

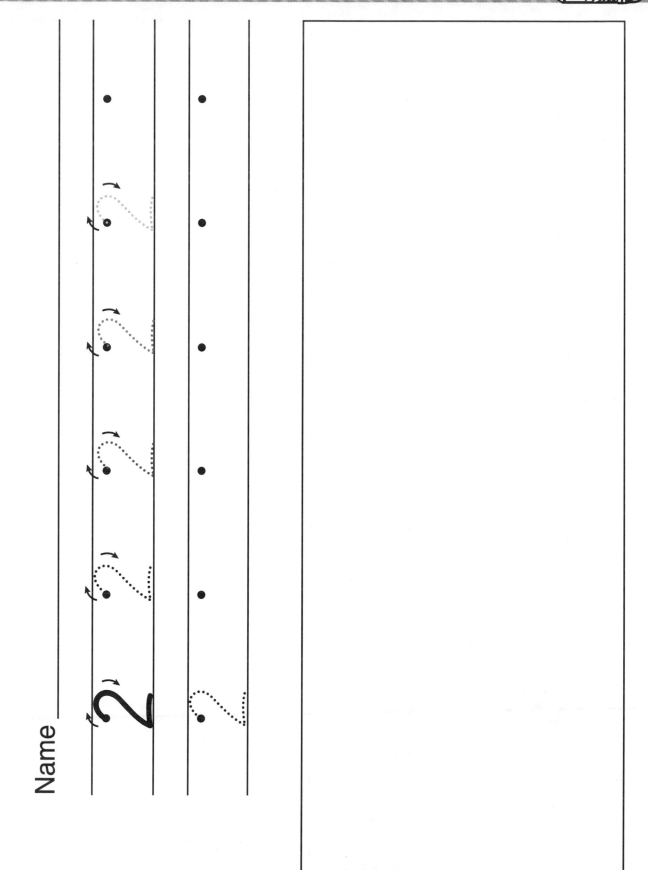

Use with activity on page 112.

Number Book (3)

Name

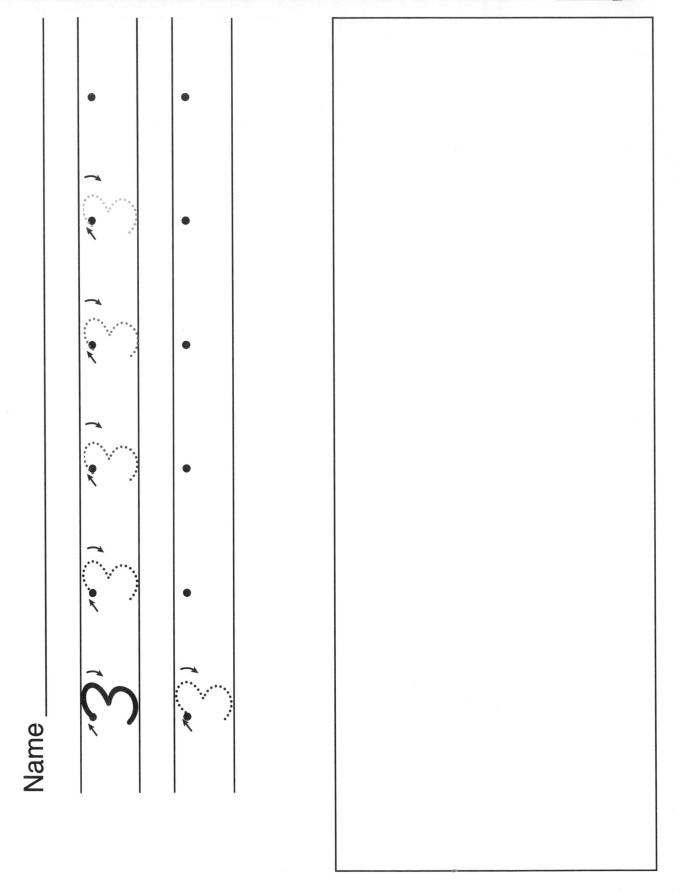

Use with activity on page 112.

Name

(1) (2)

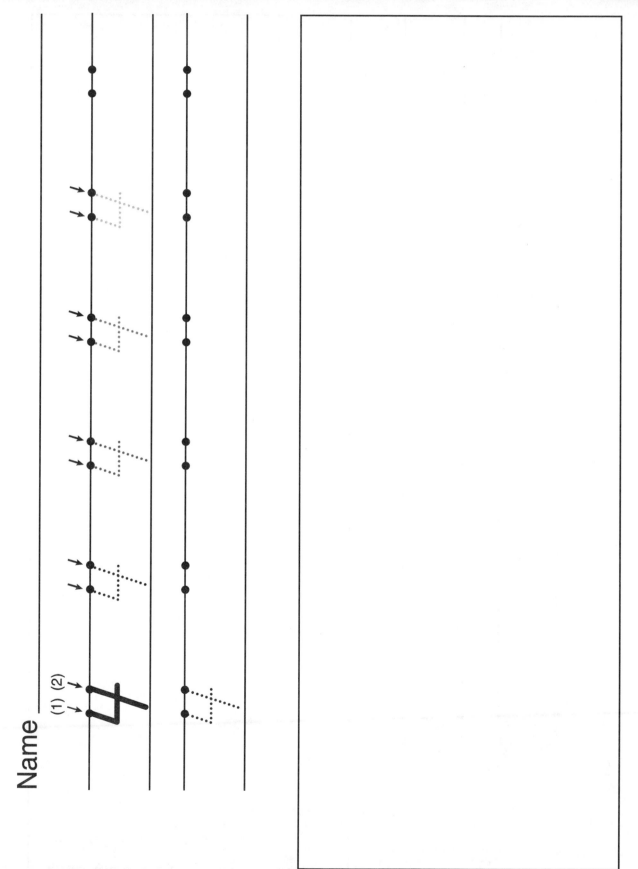

Use with activity on page 112.

Name

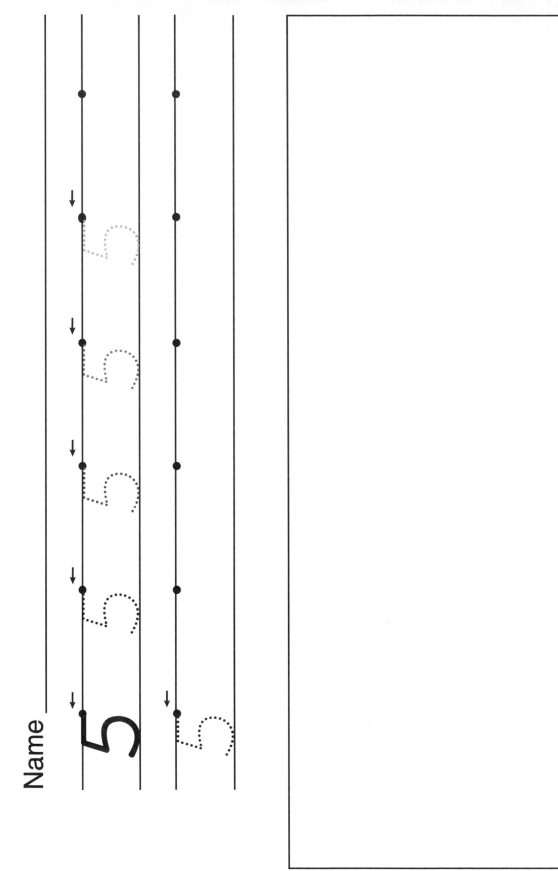

Use with activity on page 112.

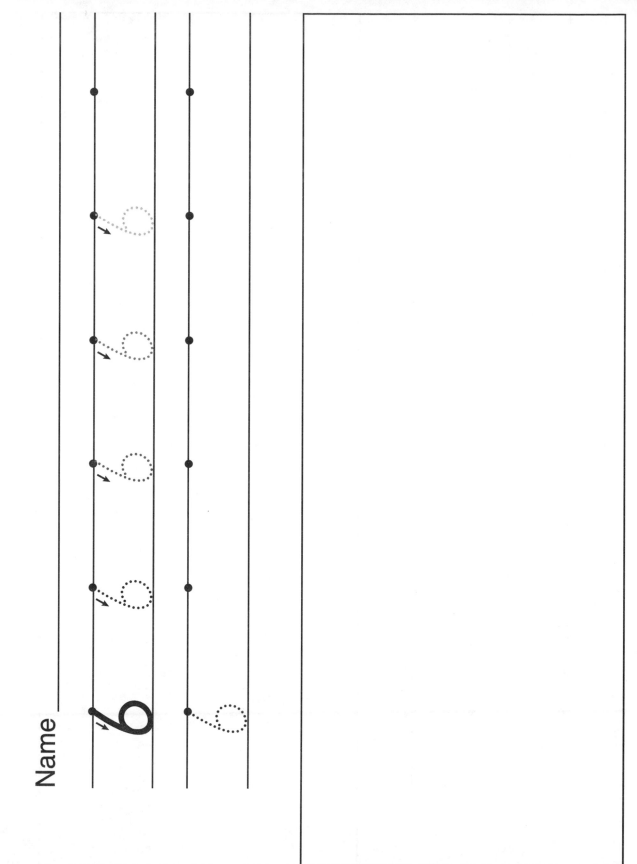

Name

Use with activity on page 112.

83

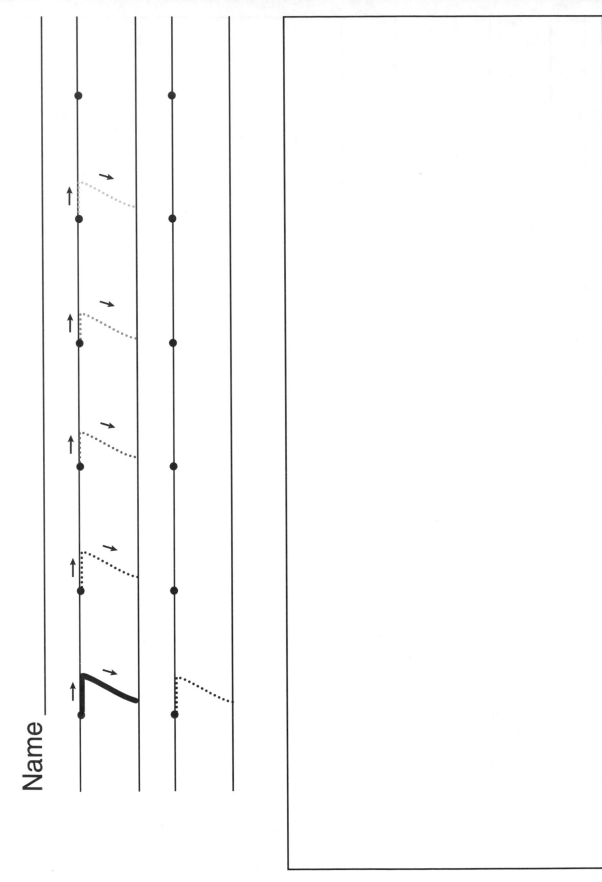

Name

Use with activity on page 112.

Activity
Master
25

Name

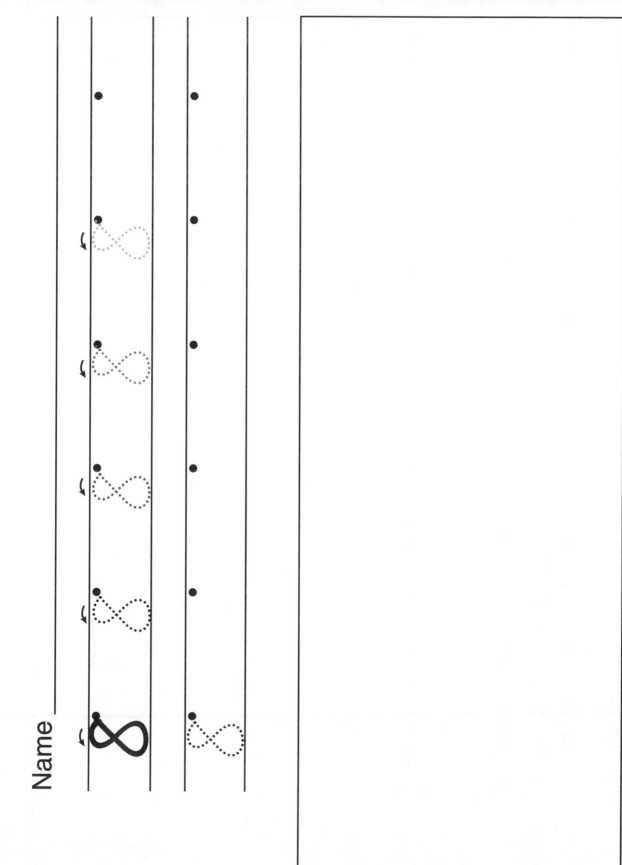

Use with activity on page 112.

Name

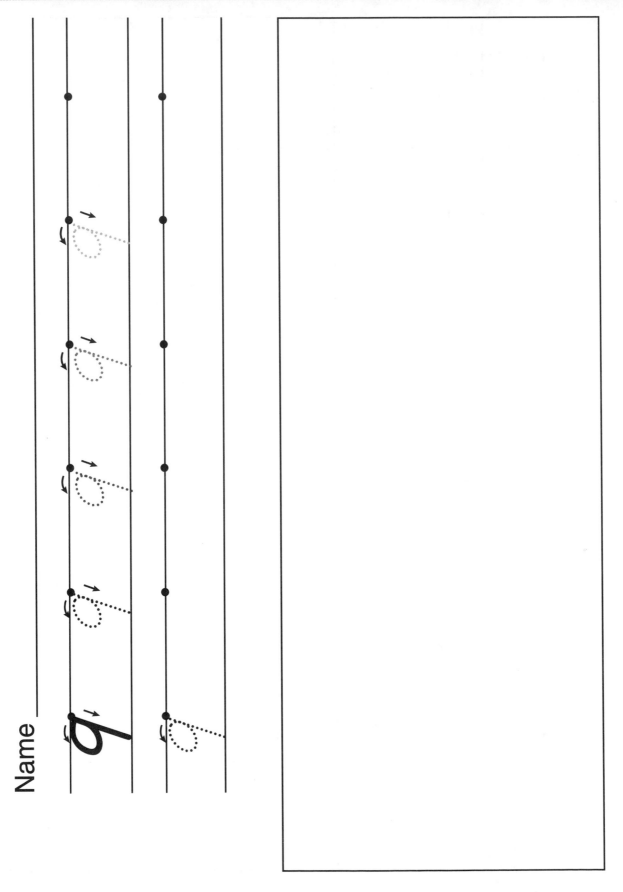

Use with activity on page 112.

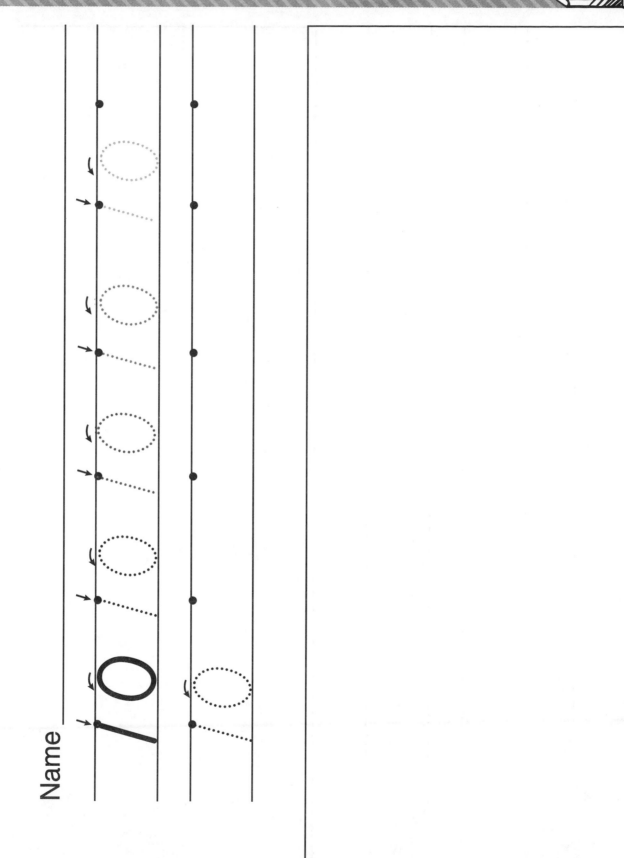

Name

Name _____

Use with activity on page 112.

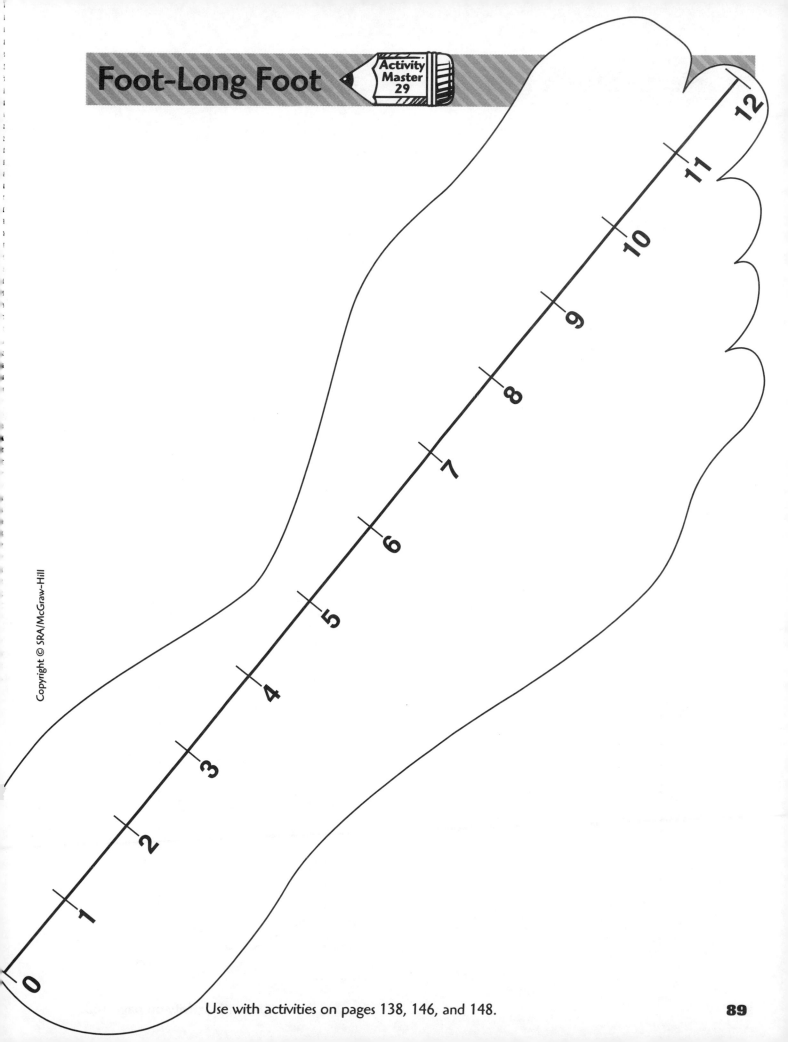

Foot-Long Foot

Activity Master 29

0 1 2 3 4 5 6 7 8 9 10 11 12

Use with activities on pages 138, 146, and 148.

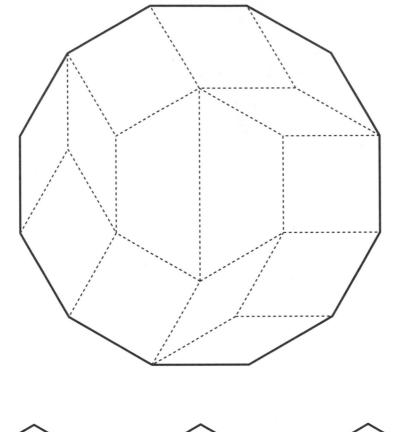

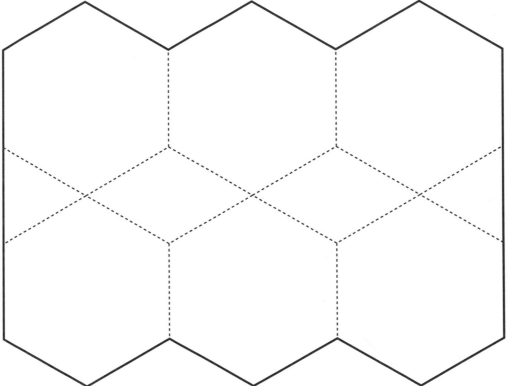

Use with activity on page 162.

Activity Master 31

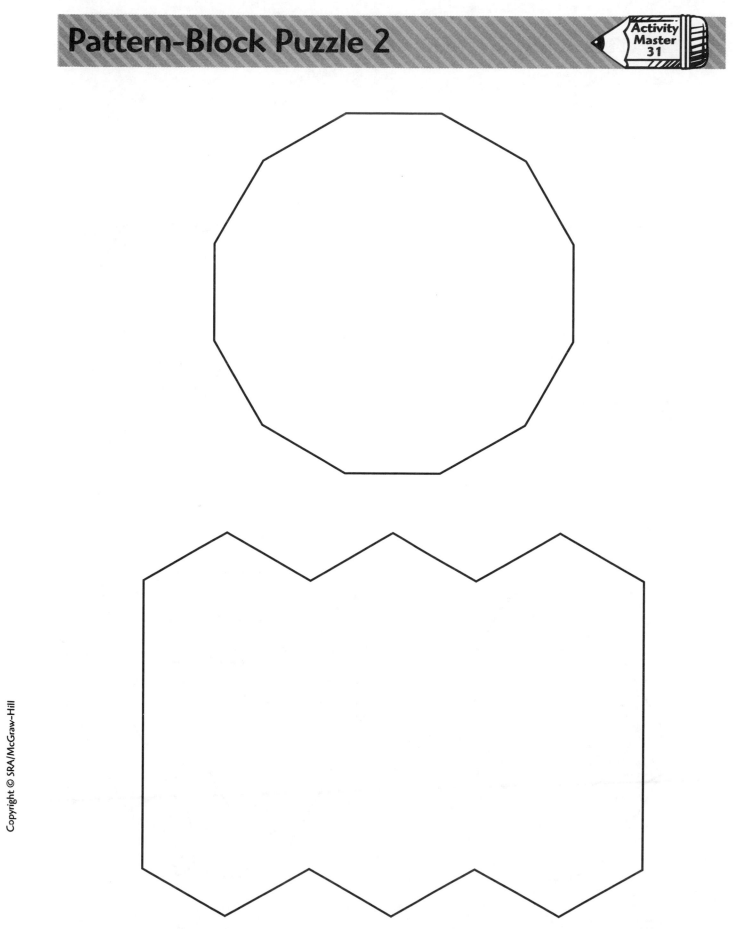

Use with activity on page 162.

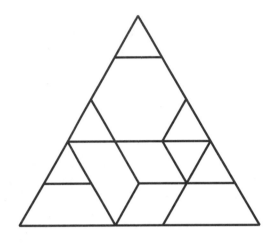

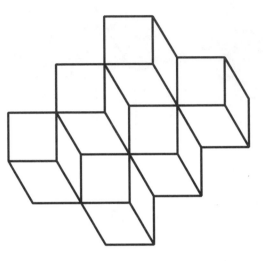

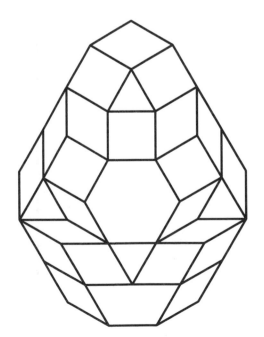

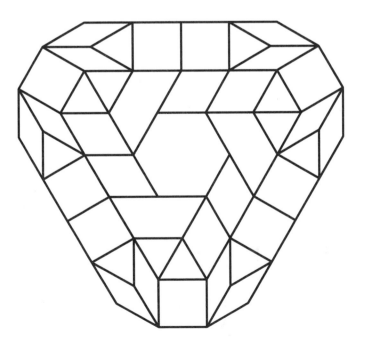

Use with activity on page 162.

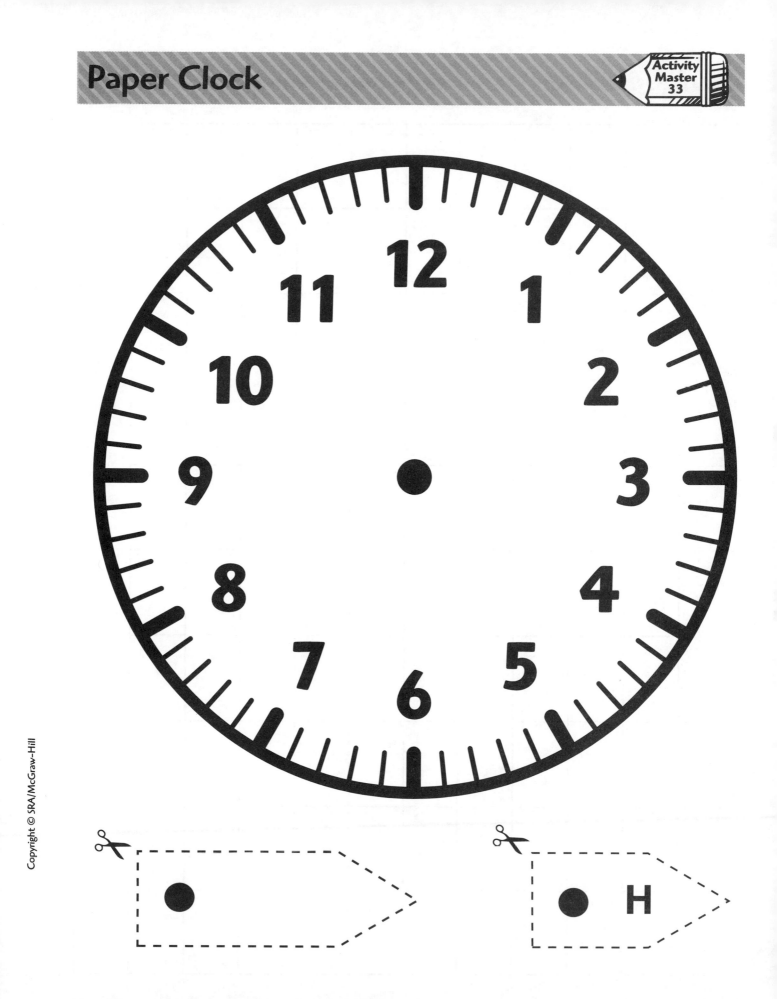

H

Number Grid

									1
									0

Use with activity on page 222.

Use with activity on page 227.

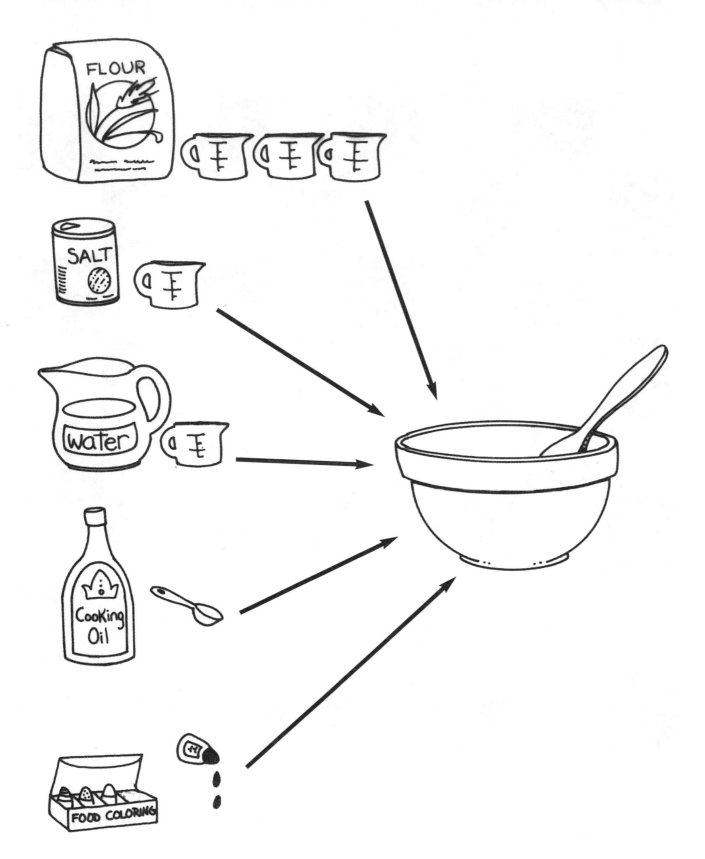

Use with activities on pages 242 and 272.

Activity Master 37

Use with activity on page 258.

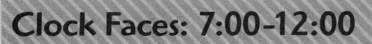

Activity Master 38

Use with activity on page 258.

Clock Faces (blank)

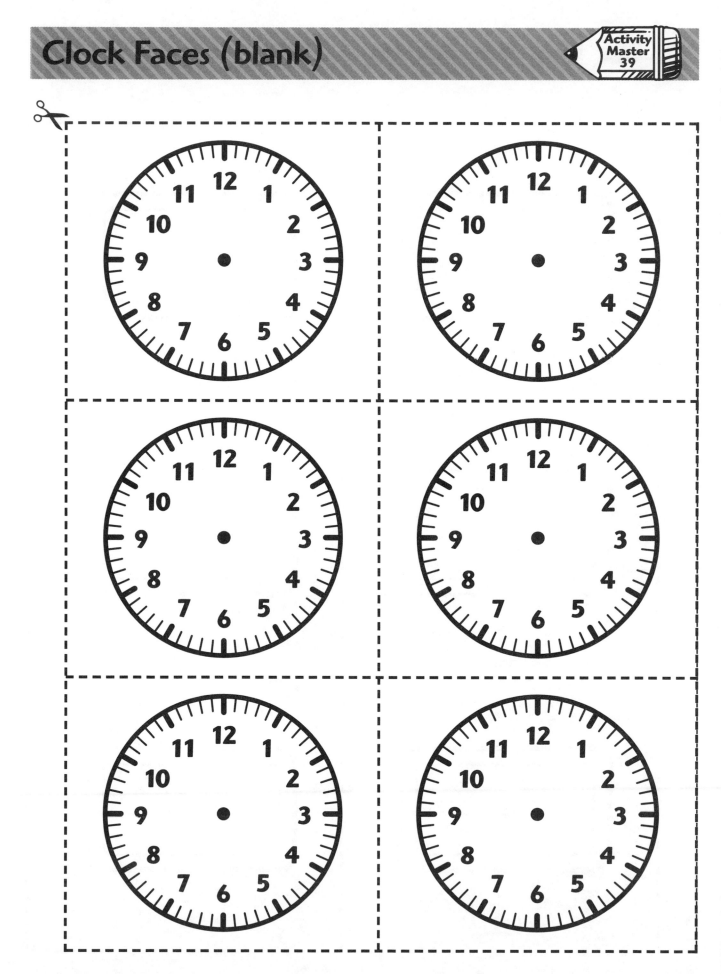

Use with activity on page 258.

Digital Clock Faces (blank)

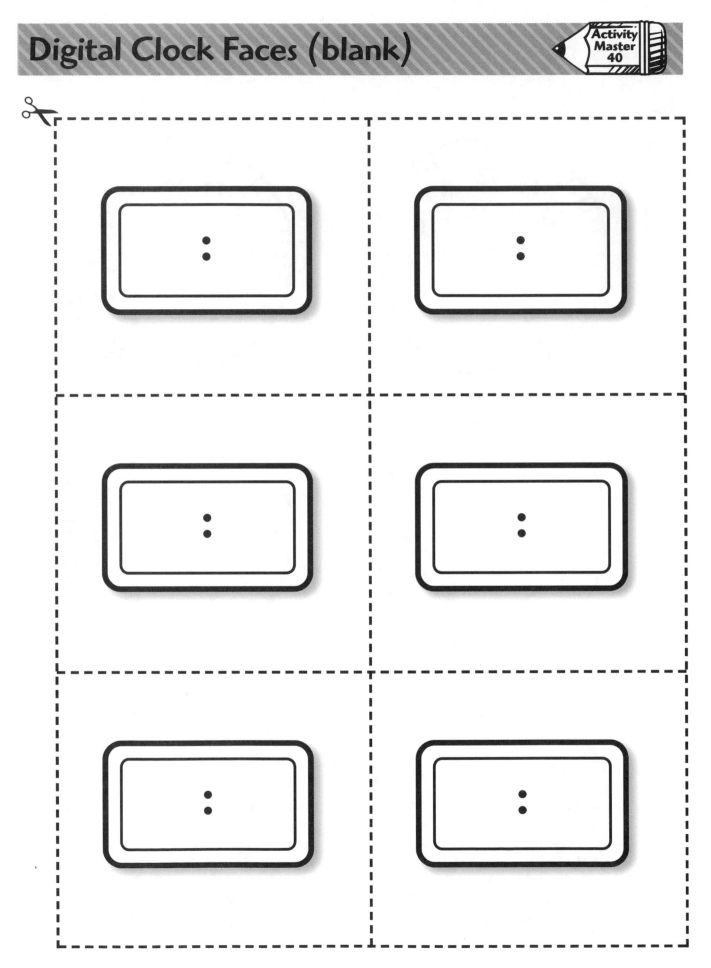

Use with activity on page 258.

$1 Bills (fronts)

Use with activities on pages 264, 266, 280, 281, 292, and 294.

$1 Bills (backs)

Use with activities on pages 264, 266, 280, 281, 292, and 294.

$1, $10, and $100 Bills (fronts)

Use with activities on pages 280, 281, 292, and 294.

Use with activities on pages 280, 281, 292, and 294.

Dice Throw Grid

2								
3								
4								
5								
6								
7								
8								
9								
10								
11								
12								

Use with activity on page 296.

Home Link Masters

Home Link Masters (cont.)

Counting Steps

Home Link 1

A Letter to Parents about Home Links

When children are read to, they learn to love books and want to become readers themselves. In the same way, children develop positive feelings about mathematics by sharing pleasurable experiences as they count, measure, compare, estimate, and discover patterns in everyday life.

Kindergarten Home Links provide a guide to a variety of activities that parents and children can share in a spirit of exploration and enjoyment, much as they share interesting stories.

The reward for young children is that mathematics will not become a puzzling abstraction, but will make sense to them as part of their real world

Family Note

Keep in mind that children enjoy counting things. Be on the lookout for opportunities to practice this skill. You'll be pleasantly surprised how counting things brings about many playful and productive mathematics activities. Counting hops, skips, jumps, and side-steps helps children develop counting skills, as well as coordination.

Count the steps you need to walk from the sidewalk to the front door (or any two places). Try to walk the same distance with fewer steps or with more steps.

Get into the counting habit!

When you take a walk, try hopping, skipping, jumping, or side-stepping a certain number of times.

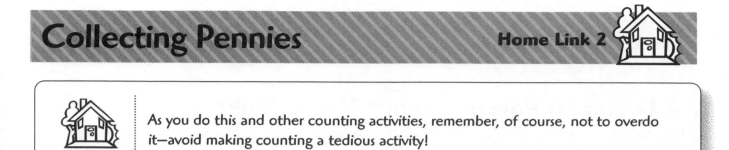

Family Note

As you do this and other counting activities, remember, of course, not to overdo it—avoid making counting a tedious activity!

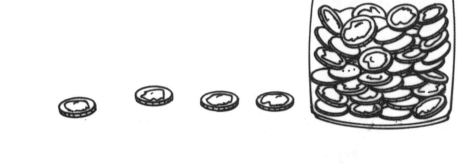

Start a family penny jar to collect some of your family's pennies.

Count them once a week and watch the collection grow.

To add variety, sometimes count pennies backward after you have picked them up:

10 … 9 … 8 … 7 … 6 … 5 … 4 … 3 … 2 … 1 … 0

You can get better at counting backward if you practice. (Begin at 10. Later, try counting back from a higher number.)

Family Note

Matching numbers with sets of objects helps children develop the "sense" for number, "the threeness of 3." Regular real-life activities, such as setting the table and keeping game pieces or other sets of objects in an orderly way, are very helpful for developing number sense.

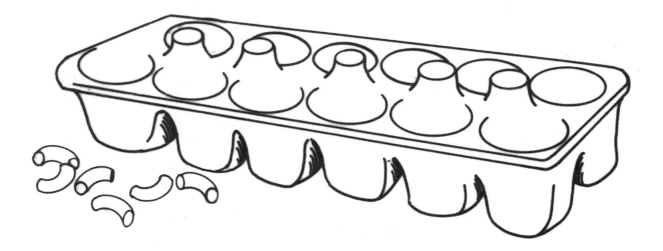

Mark each cup in an empty egg carton with the numbers 1 through 12.

Count out the right number of an item for each cup. Try uncooked macaroni or beans.

Guess how many pieces you put in all the cups together.

Count them to see how close you were.

Family Note

In this activity, children count objects using such words as *first, second,* and *third* to describe the order of the objects. Look for opportunities to use these words. For example, you may have a child in *third* grade; school classes are arranged in order. When you are waiting together in a line, explain that you are *third* in line or *second* in line. Dates are referred to by order; for example, October *second* or January *eighth*.

Line up five or more favorite toys.

Which one is first? Second? Fifth?
Count them in order: first, second, third, and so on.

Put the toys in a different order.
Now which one is first? Second? Fifth?

Line up more than five things.
Can you count these in order?

Family Note

Look for natural ways to make mathematics vocabulary a part of everyday language. Use such words as *closer/farther*, *more/less*, *short/shorter/shortest*, *above/below*, and *inside/outside* to help give meaning to these terms. Then, those words become familiar and comfortable for children to use.

Look around a room.
Find five things that are above an object.

Example: The ceiling is *above* the floor.

Find five things that are below an object.

Example: The rug is *below* the table.

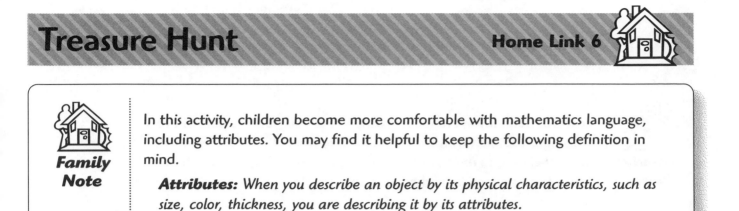

Have a treasure hunt.

▷ Find a small ball and a large ball.

▷ Find a little pillow and a big pillow.

▷ Find a thin book and a thick book.

▷ Find something taller than you and something shorter than you.

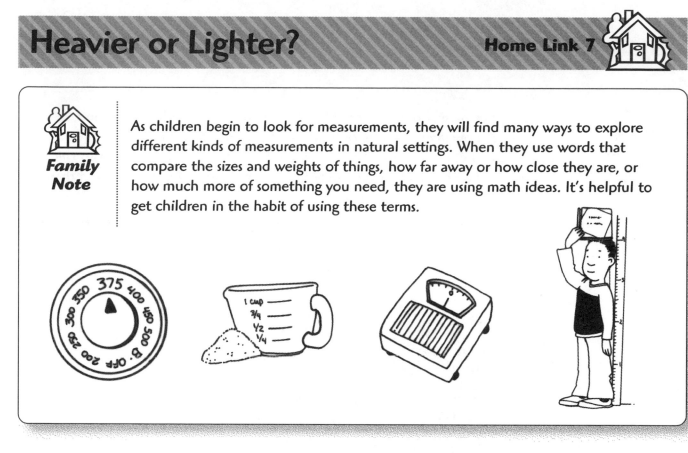

Family Note

As children begin to look for measurements, they will find many ways to explore different kinds of measurements in natural settings. When they use words that compare the sizes and weights of things, how far away or how close they are, or how much more of something you need, they are using math ideas. It's helpful to get children in the habit of using these terms.

Compare the weight of two objects by holding one in each hand.

Can you tell which is heavier? Lighter?

How might you compare the weights of three different objects?

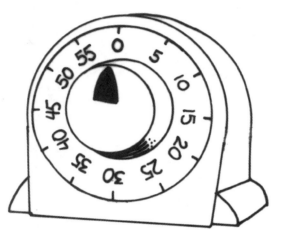

Set the kitchen timer when you are cooking.

Think of other ways that setting a timer might be useful. For example, estimate how long it will take to get dressed. Set the timer, and then try to beat it.

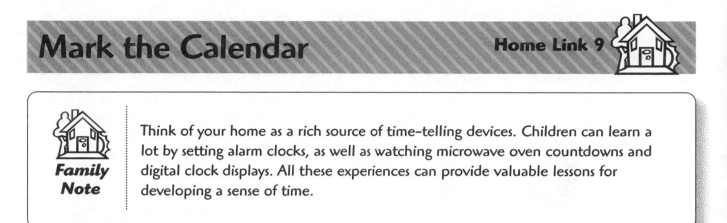

Use a calendar to keep track of time and to mark special days.

It's easy to forget the date library books are due. Keep track! Check the due date. Mark it on the calendar.

Try being a "person timer." Saying "one thousand" before each number you count is like timing in seconds. For example, "One thousand one, one thousand two" will take about two seconds to say.

Try to guess how long a minute lasts. Clap your hands when you think a minute has passed. Check the clock to see how close you were.

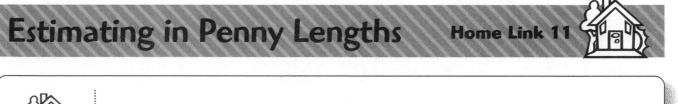

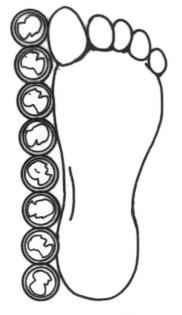

Estimate the length of a shoe, a pencil, or a floor tile in "penny lengths" instead of inches. Then use pennies to measure the "penny length." Was your estimate close?

A penny is about 2 centimeters or $\frac{3}{4}$ of an inch in diameter.

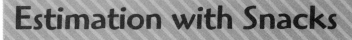

Family Note

Remember to encourage your child to make guesses about numbers of objects in everyday situations and then try to count the objects if possible. For example, at the grocery store, estimate how many items you have in the grocery cart and then count them together as you put the items through the checkout lane.

Pick up a small handful of raisins or nuts and guess how many there are in the pile.

Guess how many raisins are in a mini-box, how many chips are in a cookie, or how many grapes are in a small bunch. Then count as you eat each piece of food.

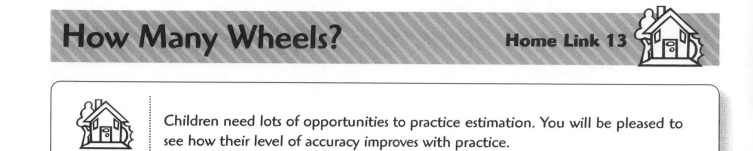

Guess how many wheels are in your home. Don't forget wheels on cars, bicycles, toys, and vacuum cleaners. Count to see how many wheels there really are. Try using tally marks while you count.

Tally Marks

/ (one)

// (two)

/// (three)

//// (four)

卌 (five)

卌 /// (eight)

Bring a report to school of the number of wheels there are in your home.

> **Family Note** It is helpful to be able to recognize and identify a variety of shapes. Ask your child questions about an item's shape when the opportunity arises and the timing seems appropriate. Become aware of the shapes around you.

Play "I Spy" with someone. Pick an object that you can see. Give a clue about the shape of the object. The other person guesses which object you are describing. Begin with easy clues and then give some harder ones.

For example

▷ "I spy something that is round."

▷ "I spy something that is round and has two hands."

▷ "I spy something that is a rectangle and has rectangular buttons."

Take turns trying to stump each other.

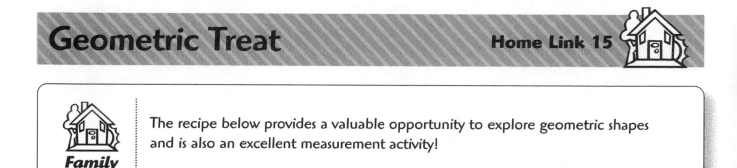
Eat a geometric treat.

Make a peanut butter sandwich (or some other favorite). Cut it in half. Try to nibble one half into a circle and the other half into a square, a triangle, or a different shape.

Peanut Butter Balls (makes about ten 1-inch balls)

1. Mix about $\frac{3}{4}$ cup of crunchy peanut butter with $1\frac{1}{2}$ tbsp of honey or sugar. (These are nicer if they aren't too sweet.)

2. Gradually, add $1\frac{1}{8}$ cups (depends on the thickness of the peanut butter) powdered skim milk to make a dough stiff enough to roll into balls.

3. Make some big, some small, and some equal-size balls.

4. Try some other shapes: ovals, cylinders, and so on.

5. If you want, coat the shapes with sesame seeds.

6. Chill, then eat. Yummy!

We have to go to the library, the grocery store, the park, and the post office today.

Where should we go first?

Where should we go last?

We have one can of tuna, and we need five.
How many more do we need to buy?

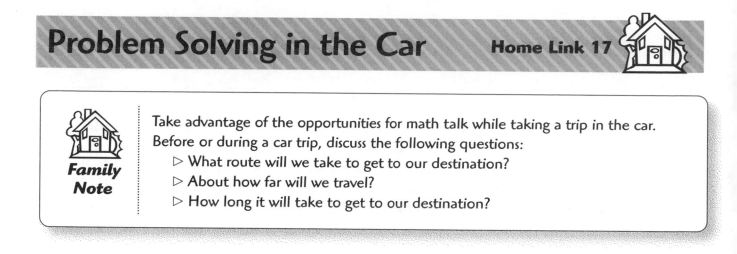

Take advantage of the opportunities for math talk while taking a trip in the car. Before or during a car trip, discuss the following questions:
  ▷ What route will we take to get to our destination?
  ▷ About how far will we travel?
  ▷ How long it will take to get to our destination?

Look at the gauges on the dashboard. What information can you discover from them?

As the gauges become familiar, talk about questions like this:

  ▷ About how much gas is left?

Before starting a trip, make sure that the trip meter is set at 0.

  ▷ How many miles are there on the trip meter as we start a journey? (Zero!)

  ▷ About how many miles are on the trip meter at the end of the journey? (Ignore the tenths of a mile.)

A harder question is:

  ▷ How many miles are on the odometer?

Numbers All Around

Family Note

In this activity, children become more aware of numbers around them. You can help them understand situations in which numbers might be useful. For example, numbers can help settle disputes. Sometimes it is hard to decide who should get the first turn. Everyone gets a chance to guess a mystery number between two other numbers. ("I'm thinking of a number between 1 and 12" for example). The person with the closest guess may go first. Talk about this solution—Is it fair? Why? If not, why not?

Take a walk around your house looking for numbers.

Where did you find the most? In your bedroom? In the kitchen?

Where else did you find numbers?

Draw a picture of some of the things with numbers that you found.

Family Note

Remember to look around for patterns with children. Patterns are everywhere—in music, nature, language, and art. The more you become aware of their presence, the more you'll find.

Play some music and listen to the beat. Clap to the beat that you hear.

Can you clap and tap your foot to the beat at the same time?

How else can you copy the pattern?

Listen to a pattern and then repeat it.

Clap! Clap! Snap! Clap! Clap! Snap!

Take turns making patterns using your feet, your hands, and other sounds.

Family Note

With your child, find patterns around your house and neighborhood. Look at fences, buildings, doors, windows, wallpaper, and fabrics. Try to draw some patterns that you see together. You may be able to take a camera along and record some patterns you find.

Look for outdoor objects that have patterns or geometric shapes on them.

Take a look at the leaves on different trees.

What do you notice about their size, shape, edges, and veins?

How are they the same? How are they different?

Look at patterns in spider webs.
Find shapes in the webs.

Copyright © SRA/McGraw-Hill

Family Note

Good rote counting skills help children become aware of the patterns and the structure of our number system.

In addition to counting actual objects, children enjoy the rhythm and pattern of reciting numbers in order, or rote counting. Encourage them to count as far as they can. From time to time, help them go a little further. Children gain a real sense of power when they are able to reach 100.

Practice counting to 100.

First, start counting at 1. Then start at other numbers: 15, 27, 45 … .

Count backward sometimes. Rocket liftoffs, timers, and microwaves count down to 0.
Try starting from the teens or higher numbers too: 13, 12, 11 … .

Family Note

Counts by numbers other than 1 not only help counting efficiency but help children develop number patterns which are beneficial in later grades.

Counting by 2s.

Look for things around the house that come in pairs (socks, shoes, mittens, and boots, for example). You can count the pairs by 2s.

Counting by 5s.

Count the fingers in your family. Count by 5s. How about toes?

Begin a nickel collection. Keep adding to it. Once in a while count how much money is in your nickel collection. Count by 5s.

Before unpacking a grocery bag, take a moment to guess about how many items are inside the bag. Then count to see how close you were.

Sort the grocery items into groups. Explain why you put certain items together.

Can you think of a different way to sort the items?

Family Note

As you compare numbers of seeds in apples and numbers of sections in oranges, encourage your child to use mathematical terms like *more, less, about the same,* and *equal.*

Do all apples have the same number of seeds? About how many do you think they have? Take a guess.

Keep track as your family eats some apples over a few days and find out.

How about sections of an orange? Do all oranges have the same number of sections?

Family Note

As children learn more about different types of measurement, they will also be learning the vocabulary of measurement. To strengthen this vocabulary, use measurement language in conversations with your child. When speaking of distances, try to use relative terms such as *farther, nearer, closer* that help to make comparisons. For example: *Which is nearer, your school or the grocery store? Which is farther away, the brown sofa or the blue lamp?*

Record family heights by marking them on a door frame. You can record heights in centimeters and in inches. The centimeter number will be larger even though the height is the same. Why?

Measure again in the same place several months later.

Have the measurements changed?

Family Note

Keep in mind that it is important for young children to see and informally use different kinds of measures and measuring tools, such as rulers, timers, measuring cups and spoons, and scales in their everyday lives.

You'll find lots of mathematics at the grocery store.

Choose several apples in the produce section and estimate about how much they weigh. Then weigh them to check how close your estimate is.

Collect some containers that are different shapes and sizes, such as cottage cheese cartons, plastic bottles, and juice containers.

Use the containers to pour water back and forth. Try to find out which container holds the most, which holds the least, and which containers hold about the same amount.

Family Note

Remember to take advantage of all the opportunities for mathematics learning that are a part of making meals and snacks with your child. In this activity, use the terms *thick, thicker, thickest, thin, thinner,* and *thinnest* when comparing the bread to the filling in a sandwich.

Make a favorite sandwich.

Compare the bread to the filling.

Cut the sandwich in half.

Then cut the halves into quarters.

Use fraction names to describe the parts as someone cuts them.

Are fourths of the sandwich larger or smaller than halves?

Have someone cut an apple for you. Say whether you want it cut in halves, quarters, or eighths.

Watch as the apple is cut into those parts. Are the pieces equal in size?

Comparing Two Books

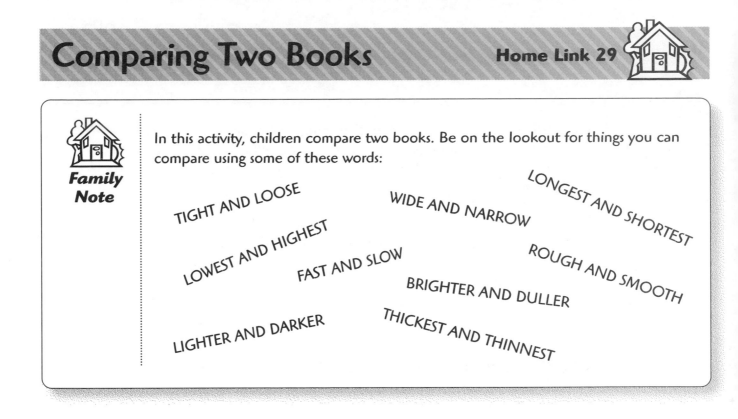

Family Note

In this activity, children compare two books. Be on the lookout for things you can compare using some of these words:

TIGHT AND LOOSE

WIDE AND NARROW

LONGEST AND SHORTEST

LOWEST AND HIGHEST

FAST AND SLOW

ROUGH AND SMOOTH

BRIGHTER AND DULLER

LIGHTER AND DARKER

THICKEST AND THINNEST

Most and *least* are useful terms to understand.

Compare two books.

Which one has more pages?

Which one has fewer pages?

How did you find the number of pages?

Did you estimate, count, or look at the last page number?

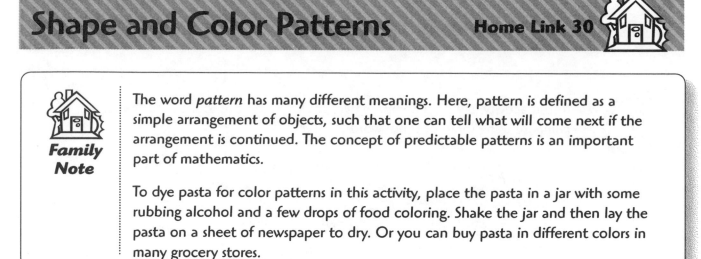
Family Note

The word *pattern* has many different meanings. Here, pattern is defined as a simple arrangement of objects, such that one can tell what will come next if the arrangement is continued. The concept of predictable patterns is an important part of mathematics.

To dye pasta for color patterns in this activity, place the pasta in a jar with some rubbing alcohol and a few drops of food coloring. Shake the jar and then lay the pasta on a sheet of newspaper to dry. Or you can buy pasta in different colors in many grocery stores.

You can make patterns with food. Make some patterns with cereals and crackers that have different shapes and colors. If the cereal has holes, string a cereal pattern on yarn to make a necklace or bracelet that you can eat.

Or

Make patterns with different kinds of tube-shaped pasta. Use plain or colored pasta. Sort by color, shape, or both. Make your patterns into necklaces or bracelets or glue them on paper. (Do not eat these patterns!)

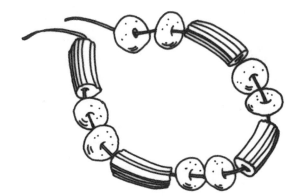

Family Note

Many children know the meaning of some signs and signals before they can read. For example, they may know that it is safe to walk across the street when there is a green light, but they may not recognize additional signs with different shapes and colors.

As you talk about signs, use the terms *circle*, *octagon*, *diamond* (or *rhombus*), and *rectangle* to describe the shapes. In addition to learning the names of the shapes, your child will become an observant traveler.

Look at the different shapes of road signs and safety signs. What shapes do you see? Why are stop signs, caution signs, and information signs shaped differently?

Family Note

Collecting data helps children sort, record, count, compare, and visualize complex information.

What do you think is the most popular car color?

Make a guess. Then, when you are on a trip or in a parking lot, check your answer.

What did you find out?

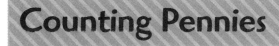

Family Note

On Home Link 2, Collecting Pennies, you began to collect pennies in a family penny jar. By this point in the year, you will probably have a large number of pennies in the jar. This collection can be an excellent tool for many counting and estimation activities.

Try counting the pennies in your family penny jar for a really big count. Can you think of a good way to help keep track of the total?

Make piles of ten and count by tens.

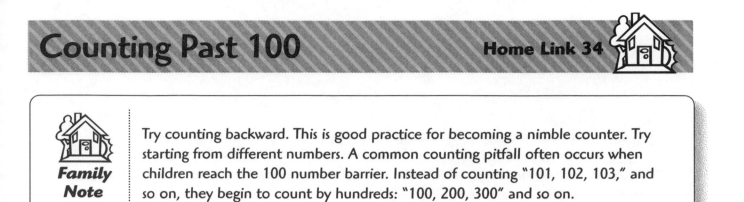

Practice counting past 100. Start from different numbers, such as 81, 92, and 68.

Practice counting by 2s, 5s, or 10s.
This is called "skip counting."

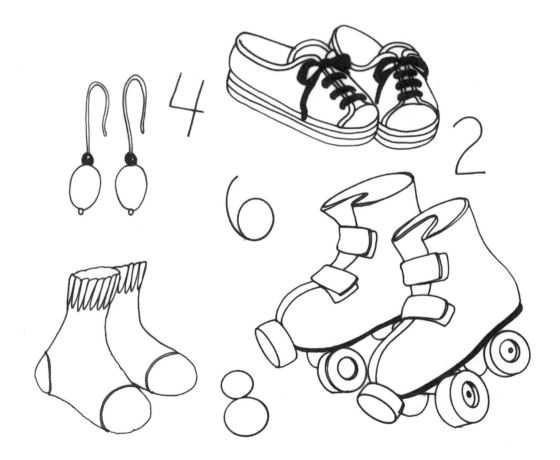

Family Note

You may want to repeat this activity from time to time to see if there is much weight change over time. Once in a while, try estimating weights of other things. Weigh them and check the weights against your estimates.

Guess how much you weigh. Weigh yourself on a scale to check your estimate.

A young beaver weighs about 40 pounds. Do you weigh more or less than a young beaver?

Try to assemble a pile of objects on a bath scale that weighs about the same amount as you.

Watch someone cut a pizza into equal pieces. Count the pieces. Use fraction names to describe the pieces.

For example, if someone cuts a pizza into 4 pieces, each piece is $\frac{1}{4}$ of the whole pizza.

Compare the sizes of the pieces as someone divides the pizza into smaller and smaller sections. Is $\frac{1}{2}$ of the pizza smaller or larger than $\frac{1}{4}$ of the pizza?

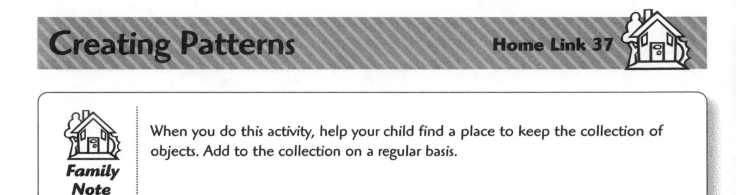

Family Note

When you do this activity, help your child find a place to keep the collection of objects. Add to the collection on a regular basis.

Collect different kinds and sizes of objects, such as: lids from juice bottles, soda bottles, and buttons.

Use the objects to make patterns.

Try to describe the pattern to someone.

Use other collections to make patterns, such as pennies, nickels, and dimes.

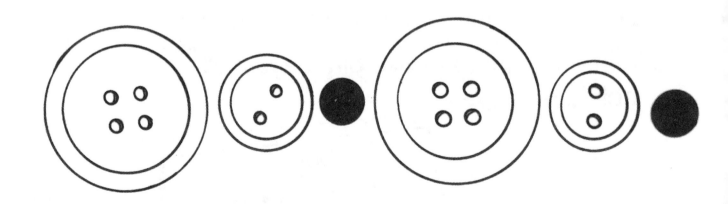

Family Note

Calendars offer many valuable opportunities for children to count and read numbers. Talk about extending your Kindergartener's personal calendar into a family calendar on which you can record important family appointments, events, and occasions.

Look at your calendar to find answers to the following questions:

▷ How many days are there this month?

▷ How many Wednesdays? Fridays? Sundays?

▷ What day is the first? The fifth?

▷ What is today's date?

▷ How many days are left in this month?

▷ Mark special days like birthdays and holidays.

Think of three things you can do in one minute or less.

Have someone time you to see if you really can do all three things in a minute.

For example, can you touch your toes ten times, do five jumping jacks, and spin around three times in one minute?

Guess how much of your room you can clean in two minutes and then try cleaning it for two minutes.

Did you do more or less than you thought you would?

Was your prediction close, or were you surprised at the result?

Listen to the weather report on television or radio. Compare the temperature given to the reading on your own home thermometer. Are they the same or different?

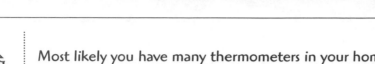

Check the thermometer at the same time of day for a few days in a row.

Has the temperature stayed the same? Is it higher or lower? You might want to record the temperature on your calendar.

Before reading the thermometer, predict whether today is warmer or colder than yesterday. Then check to see if you were right.

Building Geometric Shapes

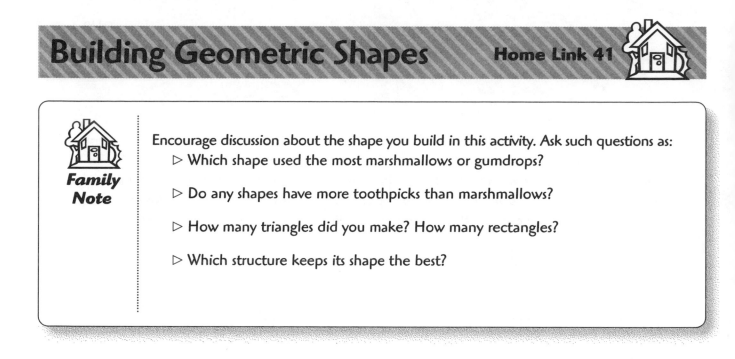

Family Note

Encourage discussion about the shape you build in this activity. Ask such questions as:

▷ Which shape used the most marshmallows or gumdrops?

▷ Do any shapes have more toothpicks than marshmallows?

▷ How many triangles did you make? How many rectangles?

▷ Which structure keeps its shape the best?

Build shapes and structures with miniature marshmallows or gumdrops and toothpicks.

Begin with flat 2-dimensional shapes, then try building up to 3-dimensional shapes, such as cubes, pyramids, and prisms.

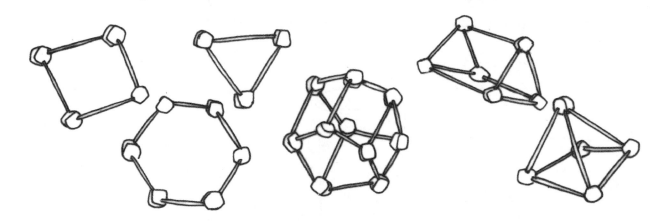

Bring one or two of your shapes to school.

Family Note

As you share a shape snack, you may want to talk about the shapes. For example, you might ask questions such as the following: *How many points does a triangle have? How many sides does a square have? What other things can you think of that are circles? Does a circle have any corners?* Informal conversations like this help children recognize the similarities and differences among geometric shapes.

Plan and prepare a shape snack with someone.

▷ Cut cheese into squares and triangles.

▷ Choose crackers that are squares and circles.

▷ Grapes are spheres.

▷ Slice oranges into circles.

▷ For a cylinder, try a glass of milk.

>
>
> **Family Note**
>
> Keep the following definition in mind as you do this activity.
>
> **Array:** *a rectangular arrangement of objects in rows and columns.*
>
> Later on, arrays will play an important role in demonstrating multiplication.

Grocery stores are a gold mine for mathematics. There are lots of numbers, shapes, arrangements, measures, and problems to be solved.

Look for different shapes: cylinder, rectangular prism (such as a cereal box), pyramid, sphere, circle, oval, square, rectangle, and triangle.

Look for products packaged in regular arrangements of arrays, such as eggs (a 2 × 6 or 3 × 4 array) or a six-pack of juices (a 2 × 3 array).

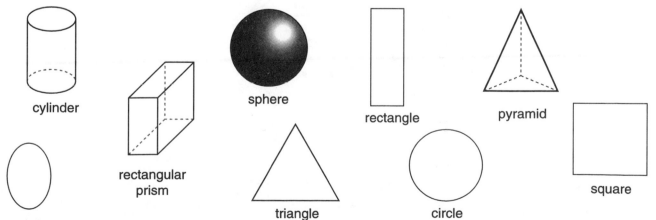

cylinder

sphere

rectangle

pyramid

rectangular prism

triangle

circle

square

oval

Family Note

Children's earliest exposure to mathematical division is usually through "equal sharing," or dividing any whole object or group of objects into two or more equal parts or equal groups. Look for opportunities to divide objects or groups of objects into equal parts or groups.

Children understand that dividing something "equally" is the fairest way to share a treat.

Take a small group of objects, such as pennies, beans, or popcorn, and divide it into two equal groups, three equal groups, or more.

What can you do with the leftover objects?